✳ READING DRAMA

David Scanlan

C. W. Post Campus
Long Island University

For Jeffrey, with
all my hopes for his
future and with all joy for
my pride
his present.
Love,
Barbara
June 5, 2010

Mayfield Publishing Company
Mountain View, California

About the author

David Scanlan is Chair of the Department of Theatre and Film at the C.W. Post Campus of Long Island University. He was educated at the University of California at Berkeley and the University of Minnesota where he received a Ph.D. in Theatre Arts. His work as a teacher, author, and director spans educational and professional theatre and includes three seasons with Repertory Theatre, New Orleans where, as dramaturg, he wrote study guides for city-wide classroom use in connection with student play-going. He has published in *The Tulane Drama Review* and *Modern Drama* and is the editor of *Five Comedies* (Houghton Mifflin Company).

Library of Congress Cataloging-in-Publication Data

Scanlan, David.
    Reading drama.

    Includes index.
    1. Drama.   2. Reading (Higher education)   I. Title.
PN1655.S33   1988   808.2   87-31293
ISBN 0-87484-735-4

Manufactured in the United States of America

10 9 8 7 6 5 4 3 2

Mayfield Publishing Company
1240 Villa Street
Mountain View, California 94041

Sponsoring editor, Jan Beatty; production editor, Linda Toy; manuscript editor, Cecelia Secor; text designer, Cynthia Bassett; cover designer, Andrew Ogus. The test was set in 10/12 Sabon by Kachina Typesetting and printed on 50# Finch Opaque by George Banta Co.

Additional credits appear on a continuation of the copyright page, p.176.

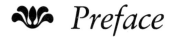 *Preface*

Reading Drama is designed to empower readers to respond fully and creatively to drama in print. The book provides a comprehensive description of the principles of drama for students with no previous knowledge of the subject and then uses these principles to introduce dramatic periods, authors, and works most frequently read in college classrooms.

Approach and Audience

In a straightforward manner, the book addresses such recurrent challenges in teaching drama as the Greek chorus, Shakespearean language, classical theatre conventions, plot in Chekhov, the methods of Bertolt Brecht, and making real connections with nonrealistic dramatic styles. Because all drama is presented from a unified perspective, skills acquired in reading one play can be transferred to the next, and learning can be cumulative. When seen as a coherent whole, drama becomes a universal language that students can use to explore the vast and various world of 2500 years of western culture. *Reading Drama* can be used in courses that present drama in the context of world literature, that survey or introduce drama, or that focus on a single period or author. Students of acting, directing, design, or play writing will find in *Reading Drama* useful tools for sharpening script-reading skills.

The richness of drama is most fully experienced when the reader is simultaneously aware of the structural and performance dimensions of the play. *Reading Drama* helps develop this awareness by emphasizing the enlivening dimension of the theatre event in the context of a traditional approach to critical and historical issues. Commonly accepted methods of describing and analyzing drama are restated within a single, coherent framework. New terminology, although sometimes necessary, is kept to a minimum. Basic principles are presented concisely and applied to all types of drama through self-explanatory examples from a full range of plays. This selection of examples may suggest, but does not dictate, a reading list. To show that a single play can have many aspects, certain examples are repeated throughout the book. These, like all examples, are meant to illustrate the concept at hand, not interpret the play for the reader.

Organization

The material of the book is presented in terms of two chronologies, that of the reading process, and that of the history of drama. Part One describes how "images of action" arise from the reader's interaction with the script. Part Two helps the student recognize the various patterns into which these images are progressively assembled as the play unfolds. In Parts Three and Four, the reader is introduced to major instances of classical and modern drama presented in the context of principles already outlined. These final two sections serve primarily to introduce particular periods, authors, and plays. Although they deal less specifically with the reading process, they nevertheless sustain and recall the point of view developed in the first part of the book.

Reading Drama can be read as a continuous discourse or as a manual for readers with specialized interests. Any of the four sections may be read, with the aid of the glossary, as an independent unit. Parts Two, Three, and Four are each headed by introductory chapters that also function as summaries of their respective subjects. Reader's checklists, which appear at appropriate intervals throughout the book, further help readers' comprehension of the major topics. This method of organization assures tight continuity for beginners, while allowing readers with specialized concerns to assemble their own plan of study. For instance, students of Shakespeare can read Parts One and Two and the introduction to classical drama as preparation for the chapter on Shakespeare. Students of modern drama will be able to read Part Four without having read the preceding section on classical drama. By consulting the index, readers concerned with a single play can explore the ramifications of its position or positions in the book. It should be stressed, however, that the comparative and cross-referential method of *Reading Drama* means that the parts are most fully understood in terms of the whole.

Many of the concepts in *Reading Drama* are presented as complementary pairs, making them easy to grasp and retain. If students of drama understand the polarities of a troubling issue, they are never without a point of orientation. Are we dealing here, they will be able to ask, with background or action, with a classical or modern script, with a realistic or antirealistic point of view?

But all issues in drama cannot be resolved in the same either/or terms in which they first appear. The study of drama leads to the discovery that what looks absolute at first will unfold, in time, into something of intriguing relativity. For instance, a wide spectrum of possibility exists between the poles of realism and antirealism, and even of classical and modern drama. The absolutes of *Reading Drama,* then, are intended to function as do the negative and positive poles of an electrical system. In the sparks and currents that jump and flow between the poles, the process of drama comes to life.

Acknowledgments

The conception and completion of *Reading Drama* owes much to the sustaining presence of Mayfield editors Lansing Hays and Janet Beatty whose insight, patience, and underlying sense of purpose kept the project always on course. Julian Mates, friend and dean, offered valuable support and suggestions. I also thank those colleagues who reviewed the several drafts of the manuscript: Louis E. Catron, College of William and Mary; Ralph Alan Cohen, James Madison University; William R. Elwood, University of Wisconsin-Madison; Nancy A. Gutierrez, Arizona State University; Mark Hawkins, Foothill College; Naomi Conn Liebler, Montclair State College; Michael McLain, University of California-Los Angeles; Judith B. Salzinski, Orange Coast College; and Helen S. van Gorder, Youngstown State University.

A Special Acknowledgment

My brother, Tom Scanlan, Associate Professor in the Division of Humanities, Department of Rhetoric, University of Minnesota, was an especially important figure in the creation of this book. We exchanged ideas about it over a period of several years. During the writing, he advised in detail on every draft. He gave the book its title. His commitment to effective and rigorous undergraduate teaching, his editorial eye, and his knowledge of drama have been of inestimable value.

David Scanlan

❧ Contents

Part One

THE SCRIPT
Images of Action . . .

1 ❦ *The Reader Prepares*

*The realization of a play through reading
requires a collaboration from the reader. It is
not enough to be receptive; a play demands
active projection of the imagination. That is
the challenge and satisfaction of reading plays.*
—Kenneth Thorpe Rowe,
A Theater in Your Head

Music is a form of sound, painting appeals to our sense of sight, and the medium of poetry is words. In drama, sights, sounds, and words often flow together into a single image. The dramatic image, moreover, can be presented in a number of different ways. The plays of Shakespeare, besides being published in every major language, have been adapted for film, television, opera, ballet, radio, recordings, and comic books. And, of course, they are regularly performed in the live theatre, where they were born. However, to say that drama is simply a mixture of sights, sounds, and words presented in a variety of media does not provide a clear starting point for the reader. It will be more helpful to identify a single, essential element which underlies these many means and forms of dramatic communication.

Sound is not the essential element of drama; silent movies and pantomime offer intense dramatic experience without it. Nor is drama absolutely dependent on visual information; radio drama excites the imagination without pictures. Yet all dramatic formats, from television to the printed page, have one thing in common. They present us with images of human behavior, images which are more immediate, more vivid, and more revealing than behavior in everyday life. Drama, we can say at the outset, presents us with images of behavior distilled into action. We perceive music through sound, painting through sight, and drama through images of human action.

For the reader, these images of action come to life when we interact with that combination of dialogue and stage directions we call the script. The printed page does not make drama by itself. The activating ingredient is our living response to what we read. And the two most important resources we have as readers are our powers of imagination and empathy.

Imagination

In the second scene of Shakespeare's *Hamlet*, the young prince, in mourning for his father, talks with his fellow student, Horatio:

HAMLET: My father—methinks I see my father.
HORATIO: O where, my lord?
HAMLET: In my mind's eye, Horatio.

Hamlet's words define the *imagination:* it is the mind's eye. We habitually refer to imagination with eye-related words such as *envision, envisage, visualize,* or *picture.* But the imagination does more than see; it can also "hear" and "feel." If, like Hamlet, we conjure up the image of a parent, it will probably be much more than just a face or voice. The qualities of the parent and our many associated feelings will also be present. What he or she means to us will charge the image with feeling.

We should also remember that the imagination, capable of total freedom, moves at will through time and space, visiting the familiar past and creating the unknown future. Much more than a passive camera, the imagination is a creative, shaping force.

Empathy

Imagine you are at a circus. An acrobat with a balancing pole is crossing the high wire without a net. Now her foot slips and the pole tilts dangerously to one side. The wire trembles and sways as she slowly rights herself. If you grab your companion or the arms of your seat to keep from "falling," you are experiencing *empathy.* Empathy connects us to the behavior of others. In the example of the acrobat the connection is kinetic, but it can also be emotional. If a loved one begins to cry we may suddenly feel tears in our own eyes. Often the empathic connection is intuitive, as when we register a first impression of a new acquaintance. Users of intuitive empathy include the salesperson, who sizes us up the minute we walk in the door, and the skillful interviewer, who can read a prospective employee in an intuitive flash. What is called the chemistry of interpersonal relations is based on intuitive empathy. While we associate most imaginative processes with the sense organs, empathy is internal—a gut feeling. Crucial to learning and socialization, empathy gives us a feel for the world. If imagination is the mind's eye and ear, empathy is the mind's heart.

Empathy is that part of us which says "yes" to experience and connects us to the world we live in. Tempered by the sales resistance of reason, empathy enlarges our experience of the human condition. And a vital imagination is also an empowering force. We live, after all, in a world of commercially produced imagery which continually offers to imagine the world for us. How can we maintain our independence and individuality without a strong imagination of our own?

Drama often asks us to empathize with several characters at a time. For this reason, it is usually necessary to read plays more than once. For example, the excerpt from Lorraine Hansberry's *A Raisin in the Sun* found in Script 1 can be read from three different viewpoints. If we connect with the behavior of a different character each time we read a scene or a whole play, we begin to see

Script 1

From Act I, scene 1 of Lorraine Hansberry's
A Raisin in the Sun.

Three characters are present in this scene: Beneatha, a young woman of college age, Mama, her mother, and Ruth, her sister-in-law. It is morning and the three women are in the family living room. Connect with a different character each time you read the scene.

BENEATHA: Mama, you don't understand. It's all a matter
    of ideas, and God is just one idea I don't accept.
    It's not important. I am not going out and being immoral
    or commit crimes because I don't believe in God. I
    don't even think about it. It's just that I get tired   5
    of Him getting credit for all the things the human
    race achieves through its own stubborn effort. There
    simply is no blasted God—there is only man
    and it is he who makes miracles!
[MAMA *absorbs this speech, studies her daughter and rises*   10
slowly and crosses to BENEATHA *and slaps her powerfully*
across the face. After, there is only silence and the
daughter drops her eyes from her mother's face, and MAMA
is very tall before her.]
MAMA: Now—you say after me, in my mother's   15
    house there is still God.
[*There is a long pause and* BENEATHA *stares at the floor*
wordlessly. MAMA *repeats the phrase with precision and*
cool emotion.]

the complexity of dramatic empathy. We also learn that we have within us the potential to understand many diverse, and conflicting, kinds of behavior. "Nothing human is alien to me," wrote the Roman playwright Terence two thousand years ago. Drama continues to offer today's reader many different versions of what it feels like to be human.

Empathy and imagination work together. We can imagine empathy, and we can empathize with what we imagine. In other words, the sights, sounds, and feelings we have been talking about do not necessarily depend on reality. A skillful mime walking an imaginary tightrope can upset our balance as much as a real acrobat. It doesn't take real sadness to get our tears to flow. A sentimental play or a tearjerker movie will do just as well. We can experience all the pains and pleasures of love in our daydreams. Drama depends on this universal human ability to respond empathically to imaginary stimuli as if they were real.

MAMA: In my mother's house there is still God.   20
BENEATHA: In my mother's house there is still
  God. [*A long pause.*]
MAMA [*walking away from* BENEATHA, *too disturbed
  for triumphant posture. Stopping and turning
  back to her daughter*]: There are some ideas   25
  we ain't going to have in this house. Not long
  as I am at the head of this family.
BENEATHA: Yes, ma'am.
[MAMA *walks out of the room.*]
RUTH [*almost gently, with profound understanding*]:   30
  You think you a woman, Bennie—but you still a
  little girl. What you did was childish—so you
  got treated like a child.
BENEATHA: I see. [*Quietly.*] I also see that everybody
  thinks it's all right for Mama to be a tyrant. But   35
  all the tyranny in the world will never put a God
  in the heavens!
[*She picks up her books and goes out.*]

Empathic feelings are both physical and emotional. What does Beneatha feel when she is slapped? What does Mama feel when she does it?
How does their mother-daughter relationship add to the feeling? What
might Ruth feel as she watches the struggle?

Sympathy and Antipathy

Although empathy is our means of connecting with dramatic behavior, the
process does not always end there. In moments of intense conflict, it is human
nature to take sides—to feel *sympathy* for one side and *antipathy* for another.
Sometimes drama provokes total sympathy for one group of characters (the
good guys) and total antipathy for another (the bad guys). Or, drama may
connect us with both sides of a single character who is experiencing some kind
of internal conflict. We may feel sympathy for some aspects of the character's
behavior and antipathy for others—a conflict that causes us to experience
what novelist Joseph Conrad calls "the shock of warring impulses."

We can imagine, perhaps, a "war" breaking out between readers who have
taken sides in the mother-daughter struggle in Script 1. "Beneatha deserves

❧ *Reading Drama with Double Vision*

The great American actor Joseph Jefferson said that good acting required "a warm heart and a cool head." So does good script reading. Drama stimulates the reader's responses in the following complementary ways:

EMPATHY	REASON
Feeling	Thinking
Heart	Head
Warm	Cool
Attached	Detached
Cognitive	Affective

Extensions of Empathy

SYMPATHY	ANTIPATHY
Join	Reject
Share	Refuse
Digest	Regurgitate
Approve	Disapprove
Love	Hate
Pain	Pleasure

The word root *path* refers to feeling. *Em*pathy means getting *into* the feeling or letting the feeling get *into* us. We know how someone else feels because we feel it ourselves. Once we make this connection, we may take sides. When we *sym*pathize, we are *with*. If we feel *anti*pathy, we are *against*. Although we may sometimes wish to deny it, antipathy, too, depends on connection.

to be slapped," says one side. "She's rude and offensive to her mother and blasphemous besides." "She does not deserve to be slapped," says another. "Mama is a brutal tyrant and ought to apologize." And, just to complicate matters, a third view may be expressed: "Mama is probably right, but she shouldn't use physical violence." And so on.

Whatever kind of drama we are reading, empathy connects us with both sides of an issue—the one we like as well as the one we do not. In reading drama, we are both judge and accused, oppressed and oppressor, lover and rival. With this duality drama accomplishes one of its main purposes: to explore the contradictions and conflicts of human lives.

Script 2
From Act II of Oscar Wilde's
The Importance of Being Earnest.

CECILY: May I offer you some tea, Miss Fairfax?
GWENDOLEN [*with elaborate politeness*]: Thank you.
  [*Aside.*] Detestable girl! But I require tea!
CECILY [*sweetly*]: Sugar?
GWENDOLEN [*superciliously*]: No, thank you. Sugar is   5
  not fashionable any more.
[CECILY *looks angrily at her, takes up the tongs and puts four
lumps of sugar into the cup.*]
CECILY [*severely*]: Cake or bread and butter?
GWENDOLEN [*in a bored manner*]: Bread and butter, please.   10
  Cake is rarely seen at the best houses nowadays.
CECILY [*cuts a very large slice of cake, and puts it on the
  tray*]: Hand that to Miss Fairfax.
[MERRIMAN *does so and goes out with a footman.* GWENDOLEN
drinks the tea and makes a grimace. Puts down cup at   15
*once, reaches out her hand for bread and butter, looks
at it, and finds it is cake. Rises in indignation.*]
GWENDOLEN: You have filled my tea with lumps of sugar,
  and though I asked most distinctly for bread and
  butter, you have given me cake. I am known for the   20
  gentleness of my disposition, and the extraordinary
  sweetness of my nature, but I warn you, Miss Cardew,
  you may go too far.
CECILY [*rising*]: To save my poor, innocent, trusting
  boy from the machinations of any other girl, there are 25
  no lengths to which I would not go.

There are two silent characters in this script: Merriman and a footman. They are helping to serve tea. What is the difference in the women's
behavior before and after the servants' exit? How do you imagine the
servants react to Cecily and Gwendolen? Why do they leave at this
particular moment (line 14)? Read the dialogue in the script aloud,
letting the appropriate stage directions guide your feelings. How do the
last two speeches (lines 18–26) contrast with the rest of the dialogue?

Feeling and Thinking

Drama helps us experience the duality of human nature by connecting us with our dislikes as well as our likes. Another example of this dramatic double vision is found in the contrasting responses of thinking and feeling. In Script 2, two young women are having tea in an English country garden. Although polite on the surface, each is intensely jealous of the other because each believes the other has ensnared her young man. The scene erupts into bitter confrontation. Although we can certainly connect with their feelings of jealous rivalry, we can also laugh at Cecily, for believing she can destroy Gwendolen with cake and four lumps of sugar, and at Gwendolen, for taking Cecily in earnest. In our hearts we connect with their jealousy, but in our heads we realize how silly their behavior is. We not only feel but *think about* what we feel.

Imagination and empathy, sympathy and antipathy, and thinking and feeling are the complementary responses which drama evokes. The cultivation of these powers is one of the rewards of studying drama.

2 ❧ *Elements of the Script*

The dramatic script presents two kinds of information in two different ways. The two kinds of information which help create dramatic action are behavior and background. These are presented through dialogue and stage directions. In the following chapter, we isolate these elements in order to see each more clearly. In the actual reading experience, of course, all script elements work together to create an ongoing sensation of dramatic life.

Behavior in Dialogue and Stage Directions

Both dialogue and stage directions help the reader connect with the behavior of dramatic characters, but they work in different ways. Stage directions *describe* behavior; dialogue *is* behavior. Through dialogue, the script provides the mind's ear with a complete account of the verbal behavior of the characters present. Clearly, verbal behavior is not the only significant dramatic behavior. But what the characters say reveals what really matters: how they feel and what they think, hope, and fear. Reading dialogue aloud is one sure way of making a strong empathic connection. Using your own voice will help you feel vividly the defiance in Beneatha's first speech (Script 1, pp. 4–5, lines 1–9), the sustained strength of Mama's authority (lines 15, 16, and 20), and Beneatha's eventual submission (lines 21–22). By reading aloud you literally breathe life into the script.

Stage directions may also be read aloud, although the "speaker" of the stage directions is not part of the play but only reports occasionally from the wings. Stage directions which describe behavior are of two kinds. One kind presents physical activity:

[*cuts a large slice of cake and puts it on the tray*]

[*crouching on the bed*]

Another tells us something about the feeling behind the behavior:

[*sweetly*]

[*subduedly, but threateningly*]

And some do both:

[*slaps her powerfully across the face*]

❦ *Listening to Thoughts*

A widely used stage direction in modern scripts is the [*silence*] or [*pause*]. This direction neither describes activity nor indicates feeling. But it does have an important function, especially in the plays of such authors as August Strindberg, Anton Chekhov, and Harold Pinter. In a speech which contains six such directions, a character in Strindberg's *The Ghost Sonata* declares that "silence cannot hide anything." During a pause, he says, "one can hear thoughts."

[*rises in indignation*]

Stage directions will usually supply the reader with only a partial account of the physical activities or states of mind of dramatic characters. But they do help us connect strongly at crucial moments, and in these moments the careful reader will find important clues to overall patterns of behavior.

Background

Dramatic action is a form of movement, and in order to see something move we need a stationary framework—a background. In the following paragraphs we will examine those aspects of background which are crucial to dramatic action in general. In chapter 7 we consider the idea of background as it applies specifically to dramatic characters.

In the context of dramatic action, background has three aspects—setting, occasion, and situation—which answer three important questions:

1. *Where are we?* *Setting* tells us where we are: in a room at Elsinore Castle; in the Younger-family living room; in the garden of an English country home. Time of day and year may also be important aspects of setting, but they tend to merge with occasion. Setting may or may not include scenery.
2. *What are the characters doing?* *Occasion* concerns the ongoing life of the moment and involves an activity which is usual, or at least familiar, to the characters: an old schoolmate arrives from afar to attend a funeral; it is a weekday morning and everyone is getting ready for work or school; it is teatime on a July afternoon.
3. *What's new? What's wrong?* A *situation* is created when something unusual interrupts the occasion or throws it out of balance: a ghost is seen walking the battlements of the castle; a family struggling against poverty is about to receive a large check in the mail; the beautifully mannered teatime socializers actually loathe one another.

❧ *Looking Beneath the Line*

In drama, as in life, people sometimes speak in order to conceal, not reveal, their feelings. When dialogue reveals, we say the action is *on the line*. When it conceals, it is *beneath the line*. An example of dialogue which conceals feeling is the following from Anton Chekhov's *The Sea Gull*. Treplev is with Nina, the girl he loves. In the last line, Nina speaks to *conceal* her feelings:

TREPLEV: We're alone.
NINA: I think someone's coming.
TREPLEV: Nobody's there. [*They kiss.*]
NINA: What kind of tree is this?

Background in Dialogue

In classical scripts background is often simply proclaimed in the dialogue. For instance, the Chorus in Shakespeare's *Romeo and Juliet* tells us the setting ("fair Verona"), the occasion ("an ancient grudge"), and the situation ("a pair of star-crossed lovers") in his opening speech. Classical dialogue, generally speaking, will tell readers most of what they need to know about background.

Modern dialogue tends to be less informative. References to setting in modern scripts are more likely to be found in stage directions. Occasion and situation do come out in dialogue, but usually in an indirect way. In the opening moments of *A Raisin in the Sun*, Walter Younger has just got out of bed and is waiting to use the bathroom—a familiar occasion. He speaks to his wife:

WALTER [*wandering in, still more oriented to sleep than to a new day*]:
   Well, what was you doing all that yelling for if I can't even get in there yet? [*Stopping and thinking.*] Check come yet?

This is our first indication of the situation; the family is expecting a check in the mail. Conflicts over how to spend the money will bring on a profound crisis as the play develops. These three little words—"Check come yet?"—are crucial to our connection with the underlying family situation.

Background in Stage Directions

Although some authors may give indications of occasion and situation in their stage directions, the usual method of drama is to let the action itself reveal these matters. Drama asks us to come up with our own answers to such questions as, What are they doing? What's new? and What's wrong? As readers we are asked to discover for ourselves what is happening by watching, listening, imagining, and empathizing, just as we do in real life.

Setting, however, is another matter. Modern stage directions, especially, contain answers to, Where are we? questions which range from adequate to elaborate. Scripts published for the general reader usually include stage directions written by the author to help us imagine a model production. Most modern scripts in anthologies are of this kind. Samuel French, Inc. and Dramatists Play Service publish scripts which contain stage managers' production notes often supplemented by a plan of the scenery and property and costume lists.

Classical scripts, on the other hand, give only general indications of setting in the stage directions because most such information is built into the dialogue. Some editors and translators provide brief descriptions of setting which help to orient the reader in a general way. These, however, need to be understood in the light of classical theatre practice.

The most obvious function of stage directions is to tell us who's there by naming the characters as they enter, speak, react, and exit. Even so, it is not always easy for the reader to keep track of this matter, especially in scenes with large numbers of characters. Because occasions and situations change as characters come and go, we should always be sure of who's there.

The method of the dramatic script, as we have seen, is to present verbal behavior directly and completely in dialogue and to describe selected physical behavior and nuances of feeling in stage directions. Background is woven into the script in a variety of ways. But background is just what the word suggests—something that keeps behavior in the foreground. This method is what gives drama its feeling of immediacy.

3 ❧ *Dramatic Space*

I always liked the idea that plays happened in
three dimensions, that here was something that
came to life in space.
> —Sam Shepard,
> American Dramatist

To say that drama comes to life in space means that drama
consists of a number of different characters interacting within the same
three-dimensional environment at the same time. This presents the reader with
a problem. How can we get a sense of three-dimensional drama from a script
which can only show us one piece of behavior or background at a time? The
solution is to use our imaginations to cultivate a sustained awareness of setting
and of the ongoing behavior of every character in that setting. When we
imagine the characters of a play interacting in a particular setting, we are
imagining space in a dramatic way. Or, to coin a term, we are imagining
dramatic space.

Space and the Actor

It isn't necessary to be an actor to understand the spatial dimensions of a
script, but it does help to know how actors approach the problem. In order to
rehearse a play, actors and directors need to have an exact idea of the space in
which they will perform. Before rehearsals begin, the stage manager lays out a
plan on the floor of the rehearsal room. This plan outlines the exact loca-
tion and dimensions of all major physical elements of the production: walls,
doors, and furniture; mountains, streams, and trees; whatever the production requires. The actors' movements are carefully coordinated with this plan.
When they enter this environment, they enter a world in which every detail is
charged with significance. Well-trained actors have respect, even reverence, for
the performance space. Nobody moves furniture or props without consulta-
tion. Food and drink are forbidden, except as required by the script. A special
alertness and creative state of mind are summoned as the actor prepares to
enter this space, which is both concrete and illusory.

As readers, we should approach dramatic space as attentively as actors
approach the performance space. When we vividly imagine space dramatically, the images of behavior and background we find in the script are fused
into action.

13

Who's There? Where Are They?

In order to imagine the dynamics of any given dramatic space, the reader must know which characters are present and what the setting is. We ask the script, Who's there? and Where are they?

In our example from *Hamlet,* four characters—Hamlet, Horatio, Marcellus, and Bernardo—are present. Horatio, Marcellus, and Bernardo have seen the ghost of the former King of Denmark, Hamlet's father, on the ramparts of Elsinore Castle. They have come to report this apparition to the young prince. But, before they have a chance to mention the ghost, Hamlet himself, as we have seen, conjures up the image of his dead father:

> HAMLET: My father—methinks I see my father.
> HORATIO: O where, my lord?
> HAMLET: In my mind's eye, Horatio.

Imagine the reactions of Marcellus and Bernardo, who have been awake all night watching for the ghost, when Hamlet says "methinks I see my father." Their states of mind add an eerie intensity to Hamlet's imagining. Without their presence in the dramatic space, the moment would be much less powerful.

The setting also adds to the impact of the moment. The "room in Elsinore Castle" where the scene takes place is not an ordinary domestic room. It is a room of state in which the new King of Denmark, Hamlet's uncle, has just appeared before the assembled court. It is a space charged with the power of the new king's majesty and now haunted by the dead king's image.*

The presence of a silent character is also important in Script 1 (pp. 4–5) in which three people are present: Mama, Beneatha, and Beneatha's sister-in-law, Ruth. Mama's reference to "my mother's house" also has meaning for Ruth, since she lives with the Younger family. Knowing who's there means knowing who comes and goes. The atmosphere of the dramatic space changes when Mama leaves, and again when Beneatha leaves. When Ruth is alone in the room, in the aftermath of the mother-daughter struggle, her silence serves to punctuate this segment.

Setting conditions the nature and meaning of the characters' behavior. The setting for *A Raisin in the Sun* is the same throughout the play. But if Script 1 took place in, say, a church vestibule or a restaurant, the impact would be quite different. Both the characters' awareness of and relationship to their environment produce a subtle but important effect.

---

*Those who have studied Shakespeare know that his theatre was without scenery. Nevertheless, setting—evoked by language and action—is an important part of Shakespearean drama.

Simultaneous Behavior

Dramatic space is dynamic because it contains *simultaneous behavior*. Any character present is a force in the scene, whether speaking or silent. Simultaneous behavior is illustrated by Script 3. In this script, the behavior of Raina and The Man is presented as a sequence of events in time:

1. A match is lit
2. Raina crouches on the bed
3. Raina speaks
4. The match goes out
5. Raina speaks again
6. The Man speaks

There is more to the scene, however, than this list reveals. Drama, as Sam Shepard reminds us, happens in three dimensions. What makes the scene dramatic are two sequences of behavior which unfold at the same time, side by side, in space. If we combine what we get from the script (S) with what our imagination furnishes (I), the scene goes something like this:

RAINA:	THE MAN:
I. Closes her eyes	S1. Lights a match
I. Becomes aware of the match	I. Becomes aware of Raina
S2. Crouches on the bed	I. Senses her move
S3. Speaks	S4. Puts the match out
I. Sees the match go out	I. Considers his next move
S5. Speaks again	I. Listens
I. Hears a man's voice	S6. Speaks

The drama of the scene comes from the interaction between Raina and The Man in her darkened bedroom. When we imagine all of these elements at once—two sequences of behavior in a single setting—we are imagining dramatic space.

Behavior and Action

The characters of a play inhabit dramatic space just as human beings inhabit a finite world. Because this space is human in scale, it expresses both the limits and the potentials of dramatic behavior. In dramatic space, images of behavior are transformed into images of action.

Action is an important concept in the study of drama. First of all, we should distinguish action from activity. As we have seen, stage directions sometimes describe the physical behavior of certain characters. This activity, or "business," as actors call it, is not dramatic action. Dramatic action unfolds

---

Script 3
From Act I of George Bernard Shaw's
Arms and the Man.

[*Night: A lady's bedchamber. . . . the flame of a match is*	1
seen in the middle of the room.]	2
RAINA [*crouching on the bed*]: Who's there? [*The match is*	3
out instantly.] Who's there? Who is that?	4
A MAN'S VOICE [*in the darkness, subduedly, but threateningly*]:	5
Don't call out or you'll be shot.	6

What kind of background information is contained in line 1? What kind of behavioral information in lines 1 and 2? How would the meaning of the scene be changed if the stage directions in line 3 read [*striding to the center of the room*] instead of [*crouching on the bed*]? If the stage directions in line 5 read [*in a frightened whisper*]? What does line 6 tell you about the situation?

---

at a deeper level than activity or business, although "pieces" of behavior from stage directions may help to reveal it. What's more, dramatic action may, paradoxically, be passive. It is easy to see that seeking and striving are forms of action. But dramatic action may also take the form of suffering or waiting. Action is hard to define precisely because it is that mysterious element in human life which drama seeks to reveal. In a sense, drama represents an ongoing investigation of human action. Drama asks such questions as, What is the nature of action? Has it any purpose or meaning? How can we understand it more clearly? For the reader, dramatic space is the imaginary crucible in which this investigation takes place.

4 ❧ *The Reader as Audience*

*The vital scenes of a drama are played as much
by the audience as by the actors on stage.*
> —Moss Hart,
> American Dramatist

The script presents images of action as if an audience is witnessing them. How can the script reader learn to play the audience's role? What can we bring to our reading and what can we find in the script which will help us imagine this vital aspect of drama?

The Communal Imagination

We began our introduction to the script by focusing on how the reader connects with dramatic behavior. We then widened our circle of concentration to include the three-dimensional space in which this behavior is transformed into action. Our view of drama can now be extended to include what playwright Peter Shaffer calls "the communal imagination." When a theatre audience assembles for a performance, according to Shaffer, this communal imagination flows into the dramatic space "to charge the play with electric life."

Of course, we cannot know how an audience will react to a script until it is performed. But we can know how we as readers react, and we can extend our reactions to include what we know about the tastes, interests, and typical responses of our family, friends, and community. If we go to parties, attend performances or sports events, or spend time in classrooms, we already know a lot about the communal imagination. For one thing, we know that when we are with others, we see things through their eyes as well as with our own. We can imagine how our classmates feel about a teacher. If we give a party, we suddenly notice things about our home that we overlook when we're alone. At a concert or ball game we know how to let our feelings flow with the crowd. We also know that different sets of rules apply to public and private behavior, and, although we may not always admit it, we often evaluate our own public behavior in the light of what our friends might say about it privately. When we ask the old question, What will people think? we are attempting to envision the communal imagination.

The quickest way to get an idea of audience response to a script is to read it aloud with friends. A small group of three or four will create instant communal imagination. But even if you are reading alone, just remember how many audiences you belong to in your daily life, and bring them all with you in your imagination when you read. Reading drama from an audience point of view simply means seeing it through others' eyes as if it were happening in public.

The Script and the Audience

All scripts imply the presence of an audience. Many specify the audience's role in the action. And some put an audience in the dramatic space itself.

One common way of relating to the audience is through a device called "the fourth wall." This is a dramatic method which was developed in the early part of this century and is still used in much contemporary drama. In such scripts as *A Raisin in the Sun* and *Arms and the Man,* the audience sees the action as if through an invisible wall, or as if one wall of the room in which the action takes place has been removed. The characters, of course, don't know this. They go on with their lives as if the wall were there and the audience were not. We, the audience, watch what's going on with the feeling that we are invisible to the players.

Another, more direct, method of relating to the audience can be found in the stage direction in line 3 of Script 2 (p. 7): [*Aside.*] One of the most frequently used stage directions in the history of drama, the *aside* opens a momentary channel of communication between the dramatic space and the audience. The dialogue Gwendolen speaks in her aside does not exist for Cecily and the servants, but it does exist for the reader. The dialogue casts us not only as audience but as confidant to Gwendolen. She tells us, and only us, her secret.

Although the aside is usually associated with older styles of drama, many modern scripts also reach out from the dramatic space to create a role for the audience. Script 4 is an example. In lines 8–12 we learn that one of the characters, Dysart, will be speaking directly to the audience throughout the play. In lines 13–17 this character, a psychiatrist, begins to tell us one of his dreams. More than just a quick secret, this dream will lay bare the psychiatrist's soul. It is almost as if we are asked to play the role of the psychiatrist's psychiatrist.

The reader, then, can assume the role of audience in several ways: as invisible onlooker through the fourth wall; as occasional sharer of secrets told in asides; or as the receiver of intimate and detailed revelations disclosed in soliloquies.

The script may also provide the reader with an image of an audience *in* the dramatic space. This audience can be anything from a silent witness to a formal chorus. In Script 1, for instance, we not only connect with the feelings of Mama and Beneatha, but we can also imagine what Ruth is thinking as she watches the violent confrontation. In the fragment from *Hamlet,* Bernardo and Marcellus are a kind of miniature audience to the interchange between Hamlet and Horatio. And in Script 2, the servants keep a discreet eye on Cecily and Gwendolen; part of what we think about the two women comes from what we

Script 4
From Act I of Peter Shaffer's
Equus.

Who's there? Martin Dysart, a psychiatrist. Also, as the stage directions
   specify, the entire cast of characters and the theatre audience.
Setting (Where are they?) A psychiatric hospital in southern England.

[*All the cast of Equus sits on stage the entire*   1
evening. They get up to perform their scenes, and return
when they are done to their places around the set. They are
witnesses, assistants—and especially a Chorus. Upstage,
forming a backdrop to the whole, are tiers of seats in the   5
fashion of a dissecting theatre, formed into two railed-off
blocks, pierced by a central tunnel. In these blocks sit
members of the audience. During the play, DYSART *addresses*
them directly from time to time, as he addresses the main
body of the theatre.]   10

[DYSART *stands in the middle of the square and addresses the*
audience. He is agitated.]
DYSART: That night, I had this very explicit dream. In it
   I'm a chief priest in Homeric Greece. I'm wearing a wide
   gold mask, all noble and bearded, like the so-called Mask   15
   of Agamemnon found at Mycenae. I'm standing by a thick
   round stone and holding a sharp knife.

imagine the servants are thinking. The presence of silent witnesses in the
dramatic space sharpens and intensifies the action by providing a drama within
the drama. The reader can connect with both actors and watchers.

Script 4 contains watchers at three different levels—a drama within a
drama within a drama. In lines 1–4 we learn that the actors remain in the
dramatic space when they are not acting. During this time they function as a
chorus. In lines 4–8 we see that the dramatic space also includes tiers of seats
in which some members of the paying public are seated. These seats form a
backdrop to the action. The people in them are visible to the main audience
referred to in line 9, which is seated in the auditorium. This "backdrop"
audience is, in a way, a second chorus, since its response to the action becomes
a part of the simultaneous behavior in the dramatic space. As readers,
we have a whole network of watchers, listeners, and actors to connect with
in this script.

Although it is a modern drama, *Equus* uses classical methods of relating
the action to the audience. The formal chorus is a central feature of Greek

drama, while the soliloquy is a hallmark of Shakespearean drama. And seating audience members on the stage was customary during much of the sixteenth, seventeenth, and eighteenth centuries. A major difference between *Equus* and a classical script, however, is in the stage directions. In *Equus* the audience's role is spelled out in some detail. In classical scripts the audience's role as spectator is taken for granted.

In summary, we can best appreciate the audience dimension of drama by awakening our communal imagination and by identifying various ways in which the script indicates the presence of an audience. Asides and soliloquies do this directly, the fourth wall, indirectly. Onstage watchers and listeners, sometimes in the form of a chorus, may create a supplemental audience viewpoint. By studying this dimension of the script, the reader can empathize with and imagine audience response.

Script Reader's Checklist

*As far as the printed version . . . is concerned,
it offers little more than the promptbook of
a play already wholly delivered over to the
theatre, and therefore it is addressed to the
expert rather than to the reader who wants
to be amused. Though I must add that the
transformation of the greatest possible number
of spectators or readers into experts is
desirable—and is in fact going on all the time.*
—German dramatist Bertolt Brecht,
translated by Eric Bentley

To transform ourselves into expert script readers, we can begin by asking the script the following key questions:

- *Who's there?*
  Stage directions tell us who comes and goes in the dramatic space. In order to be ready for them, we can also study the list of characters which is found at the beginning of the script. It will give us a basic idea of the characters' family and social relationships and, sometimes, of their past lives and aspirations for the future. The more we know of the characters' backgrounds, the easier it is to imagine and empathize with their behaviors. It also helps to imagine how the characters might be costumed, although this will depend in part on the occasion.

- *Where are they?*
  Setting is easy to forget when reading drama. It is usually mentioned only once in the script, and there is no narrator, as in fiction, to refresh our memory. Setting is sometimes a detailed environment requiring specific scenery and sometimes just a general locale. When we imagine simultaneous behavior in the context of setting, we are imagining space dramatically.

- *What time of day or year is it?*
  The *when* of the script conditions the behavior of the characters and often determines occasion or situation.

- *What are they doing?*
  Occasion may be announced in the dialogue or stage directions or indirectly mentioned by a character in passing. Occasion refers to some activity which is more or less usual, from the character's point of view: getting up in the

morning, standing guard in a castle, having someone to tea. If what the characters are doing isn't obvious, find out *when* the scene is taking place, and it may fuel the imagination.

- *What's new? What's wrong?*
  When the occasion is interrupted or thrown out of balance, we have a dramatic situation. Sometimes the situation is directly stated, but many times it remains partly or wholly hidden. Much of the interest of drama comes from delving into deeper and deeper levels of the situation.

- *What does the audience see and hear?*
  Besides imagining character behavior, we can also imagine audience response. Audiences, like characters, feel, think, hope, fear, doubt, discover, hate, love, suspect, learn, dread, and enjoy. As readers, we play the audience's part as well as the parts of all the characters.

Drama is not for speed-reading, but for rereading. Some readers use the first reading of a script to connect with the characters and then go back a second time to get a clearer idea of the dramatic space. Or the process can be reversed. Another dimension of reading is to imagine the script in performance. It is also possible to switch from one perspective to another as we read. With practice we can learn to do it all at once.

 Part Two

THE PLAY
Images of Action
Artfully Assembled . . .

5 ❧ Introduction to the Play

*A great part of the secret of dramatic
architecture lies in the one word "Tension."
To engender, maintain, suspend, heighten and
resolve a state of tension is the main object of
the dramatist's craft.*
> —William Archer (1856–1924),
> British playwright, critic, and
> first translator of Ibsen into English

*A*t the level of script, the reader of drama connects with
dramatic characters, imagines dramatic space, and envisions the theatre event.
From this interaction with the script come images of action, the building
blocks of drama. When these images are assembled into specific patterns the
result is a play.

Tension and Release

Certain personal resources, namely imagination and empathy, help the reader
create images of action from the script. The dramatic patterns which make up
a play are based on another familiar aspect of our daily life: the rhythm of
tension and release. The quickest way to find out what this means is to become
aware of our own breathing. If we breathe so deeply that our lungs can't take
any more air, we will feel an irresistible urge to release the air we're holding.
Or, if we push absolutely all the air out of our lungs we'll experience an
irresistible urge to fill them again. A similar rhythm governs the expansion and
contraction of our hearts. The human body and the natural world offer
countless examples of this phenomenon. Tension and release, a basic rhythm
of life, is fundamental to drama.

Process and Result

In drama, however, tension and release are not simply cyclical, like our
breathing and pulse. As readers of drama, we are involved in mental activity at
two different levels. As we read the script in sequence, line by line, page by
page, we process dialogue and stage directions, behavior and background, and
the interplay of action and audience. At another level, we assemble the results

of this process. We begin to see the architecture of the play and get to know the people who are building and inhabiting the dramatic structure. The process of drama—the building of the structure—includes conflict and recognition. The dramatic result, which is what the structure looks like when it's finished, includes plot, character, and meaning.

In what way are conflict and recognition different from plot, character, and meaning? Obviously, all these elements of drama are part of an organic whole. But plot and meaning are abstractions. They are, as we have said, ways of picturing an overall pattern which results from the dramatic process. Conflict and recognition, on the other hand, are concrete. We feel them emotionally, and even physically, because they are the human elements of drama.

Character is the most obvious and, at the same time, the most elusive dramatic element. Although, for simplicity, we have listed it as a result, it is also a process. We cannot talk about conflict and recognition except as something that characters are involved in. Conflict and recognition are expressions and revelations of character in action. On the other hand, we cannot fully understand the meaning of a dramatic character until we have processed large sections of the play and begun to form a picture of character as a whole. We get the clearest picture of dramatic character when we consider it as both a process and a result.

We begin our introduction to dramatic architecture by taking a look at five lines from Samuel Beckett's *Waiting for Godot*. In these lines we'll be able to see, in miniature, the main elements of dramatic structure. The dramatic space includes two men on a country road in the evening:

ESTRAGON [*he turns to Vladimir*]: Let's go.	1
VLADIMIR: We can't.	2
ESTRAGON: Why not?	3
VLADIMIR: We're waiting for Godot.	4
ESTRAGON [*despairingly*]: Ah!	5

We recognize the basic elements of the script—dialogue and stage directions giving us images of action. But in this fragment of drama we can also identify conflict and recognition. And, by stretching things a little, we can even say something about plot, character, and meaning.

Conflict and Recognition

First of all, the scene demonstrates two essential features of conflict: persistence and resistance. In lines 1 and 3, Estragon persists in asserting himself; in lines 2 and 4, Vladimir offers mounting resistance. Even though Estragon's intention is defeated, we feel his personal need keenly. There is no doubt about it; Estragon wants to go. Without persistence and resistance, the scene might look like this:

ESTRAGON: Let's go.   1
VLADIMIR: We can't.   2
ESTRAGON: Okay, let's not.   3
VLADIMIR: Well, maybe we should.   4
ESTRAGON: You think so?   5

Here the tension and release is random, not patterned. Estragon's initial move does not persist as a clear intention, and Vladimir's resistance crumbles in line 4. There is no conflict. In Beckett's original scene the conflict is crystal clear; Estragon wants to go, but Vladimir wants to stay.

This principle of conflict applies to the smallest units of drama, to units of intermediate size, and to the play as a whole. As we read a play, we discover that the smaller units, microconflicts, assemble themselves into larger units, macroconflicts, which become the foundation of the plot. Conflict is also an important principle in the structure of character.

The mounting tension of the first four lines is released when Estragon recognizes that Vladimir is determined to stay and has a strong reason for doing so. This recognition occurs during and after line 4. In order to connect with this important piece of action, we must imagine the dramatic space and empathize with Estragon's behavior as he listens to line 4. What Estragon *does* in line 5 about the recognition is a separate element called resolution, which we come to later.

Recognition in drama can take a number of forms. Generally, the character faces a personal truth, or has a realization about another character, the past or the future, life or death, or some combination of these. The character may either recognize or *fail* to recognize this truth. Sometimes the character may recognize more than the audience does, and sometimes the audience may recognize more than the character. The possibilities are many.

Plot, Character, and Meaning

If we view our sample scene as if it were a complete play, we see that it follows the most common plot pattern, which we call *linear:* mounting conflict (lines 1–3) erupts into a climax (line 4), followed by a final release of tension—the resolution. Estragon's resigned reaction to his moment of recognition resolves the conflict (line 5) and the "play" is over. Another kind of plot, a *mosaic,* presents a more diffuse conflict and an anticlimactic ending. In either case, the final resolution implies a vision of the future (in our miniplay Estragon and Vladimir will evidently be there forever) and leaves readers with a fictional image of human life which they take with them into the real world.

The first step in understanding dramatic characters is to make empathic connection with their immediate behavior. This is the surest way to make direct contact with the action. "But," someone may object, "how can I empathize with characters I know nothing about? Before I get involved, I want to know who these men are, where they come from, and what they're doing on a country road in the evening!" In a rush of healthy human curiosity, we may try to get the results without going through the process. But plays do not work that way. In drama the way to find out who the characters are, where they come from, and what they're doing is by connecting with their moment-to-moment behavior. This process involves us in the creation of character and produces results that we may not be able to predict beforehand.

Meaning, in drama, is a dynamic and shifting element. If the meaning of life could be reduced to some kind of slogan—"beware the Ides of March," say, or "neither a borrower nor a lender be"—there would be no need to write, read, or perform plays. Although the development of meaning is continuous throughout the play, it comes most clearly into focus during the resolution, where the dramatic process and the accumulated results merge. As the illusion of the play fades, a new tension arises between the fictional image, now complete, and the real world of the reader, still in process. This tension is released through the creation of meaning.

6 ❦ Conflict and Recognition

O 'tis most sweet,
When in one line two crafts directly meet.
—Hamlet

Ore of the most familiar instances of dramatic conflict is the movie shoot out, punch-up, or showdown, when the good guy confronts the bad guy. Only when we see the hero clearly triumphant and the villain destroyed can we know for sure that the conflict is resolved, and the little town, or the common man, or the universe is alive and safe. This climactic release of tension is the result of a steady buildup of smaller conflicts. In *Waiting for Godot,* for instance, this buildup is signaled by the repetition, six times in all, of the microconflict we looked at in the last chapter. Each time it is repeated, the situation becomes more desperate. Estragon's persistence and Vladimir's resistance become monumental. The first and last acts, which reveal newer, larger conflicts, both end with subtle variations of this moment.

Conflict and Action

When we imagine the simultaneous behavior of Estragon and Vladimir on the country road in the evening, we are imagining dramatic space, the crucible of dramatic action. And if dramatic space is the crucible of action, conflict is the catalyst.

Conflict results when a character persists in wanting something but encounters a continuing resistance. Conflict can usually be felt empathically, but if it is elusive or unclear, the following formula can help define it:

(Character) **wants** (_____objective_____),

but (_____obstacle_____).

This conflict formula can be applied to either action or character. Here we use it to analyze action, by putting the name of the most active character in the first blank. In our sample passage from *Waiting for Godot,* Estragon makes the first move and persists:

Estragon **wants**

The second blank describes the objective—what the character persists in wanting. The best way to describe an objective is to begin with an infinitive phrase. This assures that the character's action, not his state of mind, is expressed:

Estragon **wants** *to go*

The obstacle is what stands in the character's way:

Estragon **wants** *to go,* **but** *Vladimir wants to stay.*

If, in reading the entire play, we were to extend our analysis of the action beyond this microconflict we would find something like the following buildup of macroconflict:

1. *Estragon* **wants** *to go,* **but** *Vladimir wants to wait for Godot.*
2. *Vladimir* **wants** *to meet Godot,* **but** *Godot never comes.*
3. *Vladimir* **wants** *to go with Estragon,* **but** *something makes them stay (end of Act I).*
4. *Now Vladimir and Estragon both* **want** *to go,* **but** *they continue to wait (end of play).*

The microconflict which began as Estragon vs. Vladimir leads to the macroconflict of Estragon and Vladimir vs. some mysterious force which keeps them waiting, even though both want to go. Much of the discussion of the play's meaning is centered on interpretations of the true obstacle to their leaving. The conflict formula applies to the action at all levels.

Another example of a microconflict which expands to fill a whole act, and then a whole play, is found in the opening lines of *Hamlet*. The occasion is the changing of the guard in the dead of night at Elsinore Castle:

BERNARDO: Who's there?
FRANCISCO: Nay, answer me: Stand, and unfold yourself.
BERNARDO: Long live the king!
FRANCISCO: Bernardo?
BERNARDO: He.

Each character persists in trying to find out the identity of the other without revealing himself. The mutual recognition which resolves the conflict, however, sets up another tension; why are these sentinels, who evidently know one another, so jumpy about identification? The disturbing situation which pervades the entire first scene is the need to identify a mysterious presence on the battlements of Elsinore. The scene is filled with tension arising from the issue of identity: "Stand ho! who is there?" "Who hath relieved you?" "What, is Horatio there?" Finally the cause of tension is revealed. The sentinels have seen a ghost two nights in a row. To help them identify the ghost they have sent for Horatio, who creates a new tension: "What, has this thing appeared again tonight?" Now the ghost appears for the third time: "Looks it not like the king?" "What art thou?" they ask. The ghost disappears without telling them, but they persist in wanting to know: "What think you on 't? Looks it not like the king?" The "who's there?" microconflict is about to become a major issue at Elsinore.

The overall conflict of the first scene is resolved when Horatio decides to refer the problem to young Hamlet, son of the dead king. This release of tension, however, sets up further conflict in scenes to come. Horatio and the sentinel Marcellus bring Hamlet to the ghost, but he will speak only to Hamlet. The ghost then tells Hamlet who he is, Hamlet the First, the prince's father. Hamlet doesn't tell this to Horatio or the sentinels. Instead, he swears them all to secrecy. Only Hamlet and the audience find out "who's there?" This ends a major conflict of Act I but sets up a network of conflicts in the play to come.

Using our formula, we can analyze three highlights of Act I conflict in *Hamlet:*

1. *Bernardo* **wants** *to know who's there,* **but** *Francisco won't tell him.*
2. *The sentinels and Horatio* **want** *to know who the ghost is,* **but** *the ghost refuses to speak and disappears.*
3. *Horatio and Marcellus* **want** *to know who the ghost is,* **but** *Hamlet will say no more than that "it is an honest ghost."*

Of course, dramatic action cannot be reduced to a simple formula any more than a chord can be reduced to a single note. But if we experiment with this method of analysis, we will develop a kind of x-ray vision which helps us understand dramatic structure. The point is not necessarily to put right answers in the blanks. The formula is a complement and guide to empathic response and, if used imaginatively, can help us know what we feel, as well as feel what we know. We should, however, be able to justify our choices with evidence from the script.

Conflict and Character

The conflict formula can also be used to describe the behavior of any character in the dramatic space. For instance, Vladimir's objective in our model conflict can be described as follows:

Vladimir **wants** *to wait for Godot.*

When we use the formula to analyze character, we can add another step. We can describe what the character *does about the obstacle* to what he wants:

Vladimir **wants** *to wait for Godot and so refuses Estragon's request to leave.*

This combination of what the character does about what he wants is sometimes called the character's action. Each character has his own action, and the play as a whole also has an action. Or, we might say, it is the clash of individual character actions in the dramatic space that produces the action of the play.

The Protagonist

From the point of view of action, the conflict in Script 1 can be described as follows: Beneatha **wants** to assert her individuality, **but** Mama is determined to uphold traditional family values. This particular conflict, however, is not sustained throughout the play. Although Mama does not allow Beneatha to express irreligious opinions, she does support her in her desire to become a doctor. In Script 1, Beneatha tells Mama, "You don't understand." But by the second act, she thanks her "for understanding me this time." If this mother-daughter struggle were the central conflict in *A Raisin in the Sun*, the play would be over at this point. But a more fundamental conflict in this play is that between mother and son. Beneatha's brother, Walter Lee Younger, Jr., has a burning desire to be somebody in the world, and this desire is shaped and channeled by Mama's equally passionate determination that Walter, like all her children, live up to the proud tradition of the Younger family. The macroconflict of *A Raisin in the Sun* is between Walter and Mama.

Although every character in a play pursues objectives and struggles against obstacles, one character can usually be identified as the driving force of a play. This character is the *protagonist*. Walter Younger is the protagonist of *A Raisin in the Sun* because it is his desires and deeds which produce the tension and the unfolding conflicts. Although Mama may be a more powerful, and even a more memorable, character, her function in the action is to provide the resistance which helps Walter find his true path to manhood.

The protagonist is the character whose objectives spearhead the action of the play. This character may be a hero, inspiring sympathy and admiration, or a villain, arousing antipathy and contempt. In either case, we use the protagonist in the conflict formula, when we wish to analyze the overall action of a play. In Shakespearean drama there are important exceptions to this principle. The intricacies of conflict in Shakespeare and the function of the protagonist in his plays are discussed in chapter 12.

Recognition

As the conflict between objective and obstacle intensifies, tension accumulates. A point is reached where something's got to give. If the protagonist simply gives up, the tension may be released, but the action is deflated. We want our protagonists to make some kind of discovery about the true nature of their objective or the real meaning of the obstacle. We want to see them face the answers to life's questions. This is the function of recognition.

🎴 *Recognition: A Greek Invention*

The recognition scene, like much else in drama, was invented by the Greeks. A famous example occurs in the story of Electra, whose mother, Clytemnestra, has murdered Electra's father, King Agamemnon. Electra's brother, Orestes, who represents a political and personal threat to Queen Clytemnestra, has been sent into exile. Electra yearns for his return so that, together, they can avenge their father's murder. Orestes returns in disguise, visits Agamemnon's grave, and reveals himself to Electra by providing various proofs of his identity. When Electra at last recognizes him, brother and sister joyfully join forces to restore their father's honor and punish their mother with death. This scene can be found in three Greek tragedies: Aeschylus' *The Libation Bearers,* Sophocles' *Electra,* and Euripides' *Electra.*

When Walter Younger opens the door and faces the future in the final scene of *A Raisin in the Sun,* he discovers at last that his real objective is to become a man in his own eyes and in the eyes of his family, by respecting and carrying forward his father's dream. He recognizes his true self. Walter also recognizes the real obstacle to his success. It is not lack of money, or the treachery of false friends, or even racial bigotry. The real obstacle is his pursuit of values that, in his heart, he knows are false. When Walter recognizes these things, the conflict of the play is resolved at the deepest level, and his character is complete.

But the recognition scene is not for the protagonist alone. Everyone in the world of the play is affected in some way. There is often a kind of explosion in which everything is suddenly rearranged and the situation—the "what's wrong?"—is made right. A new kind of occasion is created which seems to extend itself beyond the ending of the play. This new occasion may be happy—moving to a new family home in *A Raisin in the Sun*—or unhappy; Arthur Miller's *Death of a Salesman* ends with a funeral. In either case a new state of affairs for everybody follows the protagonist's moment of recognition.

Self-recognition is also fundamental to the protagonist in Shaw's *Arms and the Man.* Unlike Walter Younger, Raina Petkoff has everything she wants—or so she says. The occasion of the play is the victorious homecoming of her war-hero fiancé, Sergius Saranoff. But something is wrong. Raina's opening objective, to preserve a romantic view of life, love, war, and Sergius, comes up against both inner and outer obstacles. First, there are the nagging doubts about her love for Sergius and the value of the ideals they both believe in. Is life really like a romantic novel or opera? Then, there is the stranger who breaks into her bedroom, the enemy soldier, Captain Bluntschli, whose down-to-earth approach to life intrigues her. Raina **wants** to preserve her romantic ideals, **but** they are beginning to seem illusory, and Bluntschli is beginning to seem real.

Script 5
From Act II of Arthur Miller's
Death of a Salesman.

Who's there? Willy Loman, his wife Linda, and his two sons Biff and
   Happy. Later, Willy's brother, Ben, appears in his imagination.
Setting (Where are they?) The kitchen of Willy's house in Brooklyn.
Occasion (What are they doing?) Biff wants to bring Willy to his senses,
   by admitting the truth.
Situation (What's wrong?) Willy is obsessed with fantasies of success.

BIFF: I am not a leader of men, Willy, and neither are you. You were
   never anything but a hard-working drummer who landed in the ash
   can like all the rest of them! I'm one dollar an hour, Willy! I tried
   seven states and couldn't raise it. A buck an hour! Do you gather my
   meaning? I'm not bringing home any prizes any more, and you're
   going to stop waiting for me to bring them home!
WILLY [*directly to* BIFF]: You vengeful, spiteful mut!
[BIFF *breaks from* HAPPY. WILLY, *in fright, starts up the stairs.* BIFF
grabs him.]
BIFF [*at the peak of his fury*]: Pop, I'm nothing! I'm nothing, Pop. Can't
   you understand that? There's no spite in it any more. I'm just what I
   am, that's all.
[BIFF's *fury has spent itself, and he breaks down, sobbing, holding on to*
WILLY, *who dumbly fumbles for* BIFF's *face.*]
WILLY [*astonished*]: What're you doing? What're you doing? [*To* LINDA.]
   Why is he crying?

(*continued*)

While continuing to act in the idealistic manner, Raina becomes secretly
fascinated by real life. And here she runs up against a more formidable
obstacle. Raina **wants** to live a real life, **but** she has fooled everyone including
herself into thinking she is a character in a romance. She is trapped in a false
self-image. Bluntschli is not impressed by her "noble attitude and thrilling
voice." When he bluntly tells her she is a fraud, she recognizes that he is right.
"How did you find me out?" she asks. At this moment she faces the truth
about herself and accepts it. The obstacle to Raina's idealism is twofold: her
own growing mistrust of romance and Bluntschli's realism. In terms of conflict, we might say that the obstacle overcomes Raina. She has to find a new
objective, or openly admit her secret objective.

Raina's recognition precipitates several more. Sergius has to face himself: "You see, *he's* found himself out now," observes Bluntschli. And even
Bluntschli admits to a secret identity, as a romantic! And so, in the tradition of

---

Script 5 (*continued*)

BIFF [*crying, broken*]: Will you let me go, for Christ's sake? Will you take that phony dream and burn it before something happens? [*Struggling to contain himself, he pulls away and moves to the stairs.*] I'll go in the morning. Put him—put him to bed. [*Exhausted,* BIFF *moves up the stairs to his room.*]

WILLY [*after a long pause, astonished, elevated*]: Isn't that—isn't that remarkable? Biff—he likes me!

LINDA: He loves you, Willy!

HAPPY [*deeply moved*]: Always did, Pop.

WILLY: Oh, Biff! [*Staring wildly.*] He cried! Cried to me. [*He is choking with his love, and now cries out his promise.*] That boy—that boy is going to be magnificent!

[BEN *appears in the light just outside the kitchen.*]

---

comedy, Raina gets the right man, and there is a right woman for Sergius as well. The protagonist's self-recognition frees everyone from the false situation.

Recognition is not always as complete, clear, and universal as in *A Raisin in the Sun* and *Arms and the Man*. Nor does drama deal only with self-recognition. Sometimes the protagonist must face a truth about another character as well.

Arthur Miller's *Death of a Salesman* covers the last twenty-four hours in the life of Willy Loman, traveling salesman. As the events of this final day unfold, the audience share Willy's anguish as he reimagines important moments from his past life. We become immediately aware of deep inner conflict. Willy has always presented himself as a triumphant success in the business world. "I never have to wait in line to see a buyer," he tells his sons. " 'Willy Loman is here!' That's all they have to know, and I go right through." Willy has made an idol of his brother, Ben, whose sinister boast resonates in Willy's imagination: "When I was seventeen I walked into the jungle, and when I was twenty-one I walked out. And by God I was rich." In Willy's quest for absolute and unconditional success, Ben has become the symbol of all that Willy has failed to achieve.

But Willy is not yet beaten. He believes that his son Biff will save the day by taking over the pursuit of Willy's success fantasies. Biff, however, has other ideas. Now thirty-four years old, he looks back on an aimless and futile life. After years of wandering, he has returned home to try and figure out what's wrong. He wants to find something real in life. But in order to face the truth about himself he must defy Willy's dreams. And Willy desperately needs to impose these dreams on Biff and on the world. Each man comes to the moment of recognition with a different objective: Biff to impose reality on his father, Willy to impose his fantasies on his son.

In Script 5, Willy recognizes that Biff loves him, but fails to recognize that Biff does not want to be "magnificent." Although he has felt Biff's love, he has neither heard nor seen his plea for personal recognition. Willy wrongly believes that the love he has recognized in Biff is an affirmation of his own grandiose dreams. The sudden appearance of the ruthless Ben as an image in Willy's mind, unseen by the other characters, signals the triumph of Willy's lethal addiction to his "massive dreams."

When we connect with the characters' objectives and what they do to overcome the obstacles, we can imagine them in action. If one character's action emerges as the most important, energetic, or compelling, this character is the protagonist. When the protagonist reaches a point in the struggle where success or failure depends on facing a truth, we witness a moment of recognition. The activating ingredient in this process is, at all levels, conflict.

7 ❧ Plot and Character

The separation of process from result in reading drama is useful as long as we do not expect to discover a borderline where one leaves off and the other begins. They are actually two aspects of the same activity. Some readers may anticipate the patterns of action we call plot, character, and meaning as early as the reading of the cast list. Character, especially, is best considered as both a process and a result of dramatic action.

Linear Plot

In the linear plot, small conflicts cause larger ones, and pressure builds for a showdown between protagonist and obstacle. Mounting tension reveals the true nature of objectives and obstacles. It is not really money Walter Younger wants but a feeling of manhood. Mama is not actually in his way; she just wants him to have true and lasting self-respect. Raina overthrows her romantic ideals in favor of real life, while Willy Loman remains fatally true to a fantasy. In these plays conflict, character, and recognition are structured so that Walter, Raina, and Willy must eventually face some basic truth about themselves and their struggles. This truth may not be the same for all the characters or all members of the audience. The moment of recognition, nevertheless, has immediate and radical consequences for everyone in the world of the play. A linear plot, then, arranges images of action in a cause-and-effect sequence that culminates in a final showdown between the forces which make up the conflict.

The linear plot can be divided into five parts: exposition, complication, climax, dénouement, and resolution. In the *exposition* we usually learn something about setting (where are they?), occasion (what are they doing?), and character backgrounds and objectives. The *complication* includes situation (what's new? what's wrong?) and aspects of conflict, especially the appearance of obstacles to the protagonist's objective. In other words, exposition and complication are devoted largely to the development of microconflict, examined in the preceding chapter. Here we focus on the development of macroconflict and the emergence of the plot as a total pattern of action. This pattern becomes highly visible in the climax, dénouement, and resolution of the play.

Climax is the Greek word for ladder. A climax makes us feel as if we have climbed to the top of a conflict. The moment of recognition is usually a major climax. The recognition may also spin off further action which creates further climax. The sure way to identify a climax is to make a strong empathic connection with the dramatic action. In order to feel the release of tension, we must be connected with what the characters want and what they are doing about it. *Dénouement* is French for "untying the knot." As the knot of the situation is untied, all the accumulated tension of the play is finally released. Major conflicts are resolved, balance is restored to the world of the play, and a new occasion is about to be born. In the *resolution,* all the images of action are resolved into one total and complete image, which contains an implied vision of the future.

The trajectory of dramatic action in the linear plot is like a skyrocket in a fireworks display. When the rocket has climbed as high as it can go into the sky it explodes in a shower of flares and sparks which fall slowly to earth. Some of these falling flares may themselves explode, repeating the process on the way down. Then, just when we think it's over, we may be surprised by the biggest boom of all, high in the sky; or, maybe a little pop near the horizon ends the display. There are many varieties of resolution.

As the final image of the play fades from view, the reader reenters the real world and a new tension comes into being, a tension born of the contrast between the fiction of the play and the reader's own reality. This tension between fiction and reality is released in the form of meaning. As we assimilate the experience of the play into our lives, we create the play's meaning. And as long as we continue to grow and change and carry the image of the play in our minds, this meaning will grow and change also.

Plot and Recognition

The movement from climax to resolution can be as abrupt as the split-second finish of a "blackout sketch" or as sustained as the last two acts of *Hamlet,* which offer plenty of excitement on the way to the final curtain. In *A Raisin in the Sun,* climax to resolution takes three or four minutes. Walter's recognition of the true path to manhood comes at the very moment he had planned to sell out himself and his family. The climax fills the dramatic space with family reactions. Everyone's vision of the future has been reversed. Lindner, the man who has tried to bribe Walter to stay out of his neighborhood, will have to accept defeat. The Younger family can move on at last to a new stage of growth. They are about to cross the border from an old to a new way of life, as the moving men begin to carry the furniture out the door. Not all conflicts are settled; although Walter had pridefully accepted his sister's ambitions to become a doctor, he still argues with her about who her future husband should be. Younger family life still gives off sparks. But a sense of priorities has been achieved.

In the dénouement, Mama is left alone to take one last look at the place she has struggled to escape:

[*She looks around at all the walls and ceilings and suddenly, despite herself, while the children call below, a great heaving thing rises in her and she puts her fist to her mouth, takes a final desperate look, pulls her coat about her, pats her hat and goes out. The lights dim down.*]

At this moment, the setting itself almost becomes a character in the play as the lights dim on the room, now half empty of its familiar contents.

But the resolution is still to come. The door opens and Mama "comes back in, grabs her plant, and goes out for the last time." This action seems to sum up the entire play: the forces of nurturance and hope have been preserved in the struggle against despair and destruction. Although Mama may not meet with a warm welcome in her new neighborhood, we know she and her family are equal to the challenge.

In *A Raisin in the Sun*, no greater climax follows Walter's recognition, and the dénouement is swift and direct. But recognition, however intense, may produce an even more heightened tension, as in *Death of a Salesman*. At the moment Willy Loman cries out his discovery of Biff's love—"That boy—that boy is going to be magnificent!"—the image of his brother Ben appears and speaks to him: "Yes, outstanding, with twenty thousand behind him." Willy's discovery leads immediately to a plan of suicide. While the general tension is reduced and the family prepares to go to bed, Willy becomes even more feverish. The image of Ben goads him on until finally he rushes from the stage and starts his car. "As the car speeds off," the stage directions tell us, "the music crashes down in a frenzy of sound, which becomes the soft pulsation of a single cello string." With Linda and Biff listening in fear to the sound of the speeding auto, the offstage sounds evoke another climax—Willy's self-destruction.

The dénouement of *Death of a Salesman* occurs in a separate scene, "Requiem," the service for the dead. In this brief scene, Willy's family and neighbors watch as Linda places a bunch of roses on Willy's grave. It is a time for summing up. "Nobody dast blame this man," says neighbor Charley. "A salesman is got to dream . . ." Willy's two sons disagree on the value of their father's dream. For Biff, it was "all, all wrong," while to Happy it was "the only dream you can have." The last one to speak is Linda. As the men move into the background, Linda says her final goodbye to her husband. She does not sit in judgment on Willy. She simply wants to understand. "I made the last payment on the house today. Today, dear. And there'll be nobody home." With this realization, tears of grief begin to flow. "We're free and clear," she says, sobbing. "We're free . . . we're free . . ." Biff helps his mother to her feet and they slowly leave the stage, followed by the others. In the resolution we, the audience, are left alone at Willy's graveside. What do *we* have to say? Was Willy's dream right or wrong? Or was it, as Charley says, simply inevitable, something that "comes with the territory"? The end of the play is the beginning of personal meaning for the audience.

The plots of classical drama are generally linear, and linear plots continue to be written in the modern era. However, an important and striking characteristic of much modern drama is a nonlinear dramatic structure. Perhaps the most influential and skilled practitioner of this method was the Russian realist Anton Chekhov. Borrowing a term from contemporary media critic Marshall McLuhan, we call nonlinear plots *mosaic*.

Mosaic Plot

Plays that do not fulfill audience expectations have met with resistance throughout the history of drama. Molière's *Tartuffe* was barred from the stage for several years because it showed that piety, usually considered a virtue, could also be a vice. The Prince of Wales, who later became King Edward VII, walked out on the first night of Shaw's *Arms and the Man* because military heroism was not presented in the usual positive light. Critics agreed with the prince's disapproval, saying that Shaw's comedy was funny but "not a play." Although both plays had linear comedy-of-manners plots, their content was unexpected and therefore regarded by many as a threat to the traditions of the public stage.

In addition to expectations of what a play should be about, we may also have ideas about how the story should be told. When Chekhov's *The Three Sisters* was first acted in the United States, a New York newspaper critic complained that watching the play was like spending an evening in the company of three women who yearned to go to Moscow and had the price of a ticket but stayed home. In his opinion the play, like the sisters, went nowhere.

This critic, like many who meet Chekhov for the first time, was probably expecting another kind of play. He may have believed that all plays should have a linear plot with a climactic showdown in which, for instance, Oedipus faces the truth, Hamlet kills the king, or Tartuffe is brought to justice. This is the way it had always been, and this is what our critic and Broadway audiences of that day expected. The conflict between Chekhov and the critic could be formulated as follows:

> The critic **wanted** to see a play that followed the old rules, **but** Chekhov said he wanted to show *"life as it is, not on stilts,"* and so he made up new rules.

Theatre audiences, playwrights, and producers have now assimilated Chekhov's new rules and applied them not only to theatre but to movies and television. Unstilted, nonlinear, life-as-it-is drama can be found everywhere, from fast-food commercials to the Broadway stage.

Chekhov was not changing the rules just for the sake of change. More than simply a mechanism, plot implies a view of life. "Linear" means that things happen sequentially. In a linear play, human behavior is presented as purposeful, objectives are relentlessly pursued, tension builds steadily and is released in a climax, and everything is settled at the end. But what if we want to show, instead, that human purpose is indefinable or inconsistent, that people may be unaware of the obstacles in their lives, and that showdowns settle nothing?

❧ *Two Kinds of Plot*

LINEAR	MOSAIC
cause and effect	theme and variations
arrow	circle
ladder	carousel
classical symphony	jazz improvisation
portrait	collage
story	mood
answers	questions
detective novel	picture puzzle
sitcom	MTV
protagonist	ensemble
climax	anticlimax
explosion	implosion

The quickest way to tell what kind of plot the author is using is by feel. The above chart tries to give an idea of what linear and mosaic plots feel like in contrast to one another. Feelings about the plot can also be verified and educated through analysis. As a general rule, classical drama is linear. Modern drama can be either linear or mosaic or a mixture of the two.

Chekhov's answer was to discard the linear plot and adopt the mosaic method of writing drama. The word *mosaic,* used in this context, is intended to express a process whereby a series of seemingly random images of action accumulate, by the final curtain, into a finely detailed composite impression. This impression seems to come together effortlessly, without the cause-and-effect structure of the linear plot. Situations simmer beneath the surface, and conflicts are only partly visible. Generally, there is no protagonist but, rather, an ensemble of characters. Climactic recognition scenes do not disrupt the human occasions. Catastrophic events produce neither climax nor showdown but are simply part of a larger pattern. In Chekhov's *The Three Sisters,* for instance, one of the characters is killed offstage in a duel, but the news of his death blends into the general conversation. In *The Cherry Orchard,* an old servant is carelessly left behind to die as the family moves on to a new life. In *The Sea Gull,* a character kills himself offstage, but the incident is hushed up, and the curtain falls before the assembled company finds out. Whatever happens, life goes on.

Although Chekhov's place in modern drama is an important one, he is not the only author to have developed a new way of telling the dramatic story.

Among many others, Swedish playwright August Strindberg also experimented with new kinds of plot in such plays as *The Ghost Sonata*. Chekhov's mosaic drama is examined in more detail in chapter 15, and *The Ghost Sonata* is discussed in chapter 16.

Character

The word *character* has several meanings. We say someone is "a character" when we mean that person is unusual, peculiar, or unique in some way. We say someone is "lacking in character" when we mean the person is weak, dependent, or not to be trusted. Employers give employees "character references," which testify to their honesty, integrity, and predictability. Lawyers call on "character witnesses" to testify to the same kind of thing.

Used in these ways, the word refers to some more or less fixed state of being. In drama, however, character is not static, but in motion. What Walter Younger wants and how he struggles against obstacles are what bring his character alive. Mama Younger's dramatic life comes from how she uses her strength and conviction to resist and mold Walter's striving. Characters may describe themselves or be described by other characters or the author. But such descriptions should not be wholly trusted. In order to make the best empathic connection, we have to experience a character in action. The way to do this is to connect with what the character *does* about what he or she *wants*. When we do this we are actually creating the character's behavior in our imaginations. We are investing that character with pieces of our own reality. While the life of a dramatic character is to be found in the reader's connection with what the character wants and does, this life is conditioned by certain permanent features and circumstances. Walter Younger is a black man with a wife and child and a dead-end job as a chauffeur. Mama Younger is the head of a family with a proud tradition of honorable struggle against slavery and poverty. These features provide the background against which we see Mama and Walter in action. Gender, age, race, and socioeconomic status provide a background for character action, just as setting, occasion, and situation furnish a background for dramatic action as a whole.

Empathic connection with dramatic characters can be aided and supplemented by adapting the conflict formula as follows:

(Character) is (background) who wants / does (action).

For example:

Walter Younger is *a black man in his middle thirties with a family and no future* who wants *to amount to something, first by trying to make money and then by standing up for what he believes in.*

Or:

> *Raina Petkoff* **is** *the twenty-three-year-old daughter of a somewhat pretentious middle-class family committed to romantic idealism in life, love, and war* **who wants** *to live life as fully as possible by pretending she is the heroine of a romantic novel but discovers that reality is more satisfying in the long run.*

We can apply this formula to any character in drama who particularly interests or puzzles us. Remember that action implies confict; there is something that stands in the way of what the character wants. What the character does about this conflict is the character's action. Character action need not be aggressive, as the word *action* implies; it may also be passive, as in thinking or waiting. Nor are actions always brilliant and successful. An action which fails or is foolish or irrational is still an action.

Yet another approach to understanding character is to look for what motivates the action, in other words, find out *why* dramatic characters want what they want and do what they do. One way to go about this is to ask, Where does it hurt? Action is often provoked by pain or, at least, discomfort. To relieve the pain, the characters act to get rid of something unwanted or to get something they don't have. Willy Loman is in great pain because he does not have what he has wanted all his life: a feeling of unconditional and transcendent success. He also feels that what he does have—a paid-up mortgage, a loving wife, and an opportunity for a modest retirement—are signs of disastrous failure. This pain motivates his actions. Pain can also be an ingredient in the motivations of comparatively light-hearted characters. In *The Importance of Being Earnest,* Jack is in pain because he cannot marry Gwendolen.

Sometimes this kind of motivating pain is expressed in the script, and sometimes we have to imagine it. It is a good idea, when working with motivation, to remember that dramatic characters are like real people, and so we can't always know the *why* of their behavior. When in doubt, watch what they *do.*

The World of the Play

A play is a model of the human world. Pick up a script and open it to the cast of characters. A sixty-second examination of the page will tell much about the people you will meet when you read the play. The center of this world is often a family. It may be American, French, Russian, or Bulgarian. It may be a family of the here and now or the way-back-then. It may even be a royal family of great political or even cosmic significance: King Oedipus is looked on as the father and saviour of all the people of Thebes. Prince Hamlet is stalking his uncle, a man who is not only his father's murderer and his mother's husband but an anointed king, whose person is sacred and whose downfall will alter the

---

❧ *Is Character an Illusion?*

What is character? "In the theatre," say the authors of *A Practical Handbook for the Actor,* "character is an illusion created by the words and given circumstances supplied by the playwright and the physical actions of the actor."* We can modify this definition and say that, in reading drama, character is an illusion created by the interplay of the reader's imagination and empathy and the images of action found in the script. The illusory dramatic character differs from the character of the reader in an interesting way. When the play is over, the dramatic character has a definite and completed shape, but the reader's character is still in process. The play *Six Characters in Search of an Author,* by the Italian playwright Luigi Pirandello, investigates this idea.

*Melissa Bruder *et al.,* *A Practical Handbook for the Actor* (New York: Random House).

---

fate of Denmark. At the other end of the scale, much contemporary drama reduces the world to two isolated people, often representing a failed or potential family. Most cast lists, however, describe a dramatic world somewhere between a whole kingdom and the lonely twosome.

If we open the script at random, we find the characters of the play already enmeshed in the plot. Put the script back on the shelf and open it again an hour, a day, a year later and they'll still be there, wanting things, grappling with obstacles, facing or avoiding the truth. When we invest them with our own reality, the fictional characters of the play are always alive, and the plot is always in motion.

8 ❧ *Resolution and Meaning*

> MISS PRISM: Do not speak slightingly of the
> three-volume novel, Cecily. I wrote one
> myself in earlier days.
> CECILY: Did you really, Miss Prism? How
> wonderfully clever you are! I hope it did
> not end happily? I don't like novels that
> end happily. They depress me so much.
> MISS PRISM: The good ended happily, and the
> bad unhappily. That is what Fiction means.
> —*The Importance of Being Earnest*

By resolution we mean the last thing the audience sees or the reader imagines—the final image of the play. It contains the results of all conflict and recognition and the completion of all plot and character. Resolution also implies some vision of the future for the world of the play. In classical or traditional plays all the characters fill the dramatic space to signify the new composition of this world. In modern plays the final image may be of a solitary character or even the setting alone. Whatever the contents of this image, it completes the picture of human life intended by the play and returns the reader to the real world. As we assimilate this total picture into our lives, we create for ourselves the meaning of the play.

Certain kinds of resolution go with certain types, or genres, of play. A brief historical survey of the development of dramatic genres will prepare us to understand the basic kinds of resolution.

The two most important dramatic genres of classical times were comedy and tragedy. The Greeks, who performed the two at separate dramatic festivals, felt that their comic and tragic poets were inspired by different Muses: Thalia inspired comedy and Melpomene, tragedy. In the time of Shakespeare, too, comedy was a clearly different kind of play from tragedy (although during this time other types of play, such as histories and romances, began to rival the two major genres). Seventeenth-century English and European dramatists attempted to codify and preserve what they thought was the essence of Greek and Roman drama. This effort, neoclassicism, produced comedy of manners and heroic tragedy.

Although traditional comedy and tragedy were still alive in the eighteenth century, this period also saw the invention of a "middle genre," which combined comedy and tragedy. This genre came to be called *drama*, the word we use today to include all types of play. Drama, then, means two things:

a type of literature, written for performance, and distinct from poetry and fiction; and a kind of play developed in the last two hundred years, with elements of comedy and tragedy but distinct from both. In the hands of Ibsen, Chekhov, and other modern masters, drama came to mean realistic drama. The modern era also saw the development of such antirealistic forms as expressionism and absurdism.

In this chapter, we distinguish between the resolution of traditional comedy, begun in classical times and still in use today, and the resolution of classical tragedy, rare in modern drama. In addition to these two more or less usual resolutions, we look at some important variations, including the *deus ex machina,* resolution by anticlimax, and the didactic ending. Distinctions between realism and antirealism are dealt with in Part Four.

The resolutions of classical comedy and tragedy are *conventions—* something everyone agrees on beforehand. Playwrights, actors, and audiences knew how they wanted their drama to end because they knew what they wanted it to mean. Classical drama begins at the point where an ideal world is threatened or out of balance and ends when the threat is removed, balance is restored, and the ideal world is renewed and reaffirmed. There are, of course, major differences between comic and tragic resolutions. But they do have this in common: they both celebrate the creation or restoration of individual, social, and cosmic balance through human struggle.

The Resolution of Comedy

In Bella and Samuel Spewack's 1935 comedy, *Boy Meets Girl,* Hollywood screenwriter J. Carlyle Benson sums up the traditional comic plot in a simple formula: "Boy meets girl. Boy loses girl. Boy gets girl." This formula has surprisingly wide application. It describes a fundamental aspect of most comedy written since the time of the Greek playwright Menander (342–292 B.C.), including the comedies of Shakespeare, Molière, Bernard Shaw, Oscar Wilde, Noel Coward, and Neil Simon.

"Benson's law," however, does not give an adequate idea of the richness of the comic resolution, when boy finally gets girl. Whatever happens along the way, we know the comedy will end with one or more pairs of lovers, and perhaps their elders, their servants, and their neighbors (whatever combination is appropriate to the historical period and social level of the play), assembled in the dramatic space in anticipation of a wedding and a life happy ever after. This resolution celebrates love, prosperity, sanity, and renewal. Like a real-life wedding, it is not meant to remind us of everyday reality, but of our highest hopes for the future.

Historically speaking, *The Importance of Being Earnest* was written at the beginning of the modern era and was, in fact, reviewed by Bernard Shaw, one of the founders of modern drama. Shaw, who called Wilde's work "an old new play," was himself the author of many boy-meet-girl comedies, including *Arms and the Man.* But although technically a modern play, *Earnest* can serve as a model of the comic plot and resolution. Jack and Algernon love Gwendolen and Cecily; they have met their girls. But, because Lady Bracknell will not consent to Jack's marrying her daughter, and because Gwendolen will not marry anyone whose name is not Ernest, and because Jack will not allow his ward, Cecily, to marry Algernon unless Lady Bracknell lets Gwendolen marry him, it looks like the boys will lose the girls. This knotty conflict is resolved when Lady Bracknell discovers that Cecily has money and Jack discovers that his name really *is* Ernest. "Gwendolen," he declares at the moment of recognition, "it is a terrible thing for a man to find out suddenly that all his life he has been speaking nothing but the truth." And boys all get girls, as three couples (the two pairs of young lovers and Miss Prism and Dr. Chasuble) embrace in the final tableau.

Although the motto of comedy is Love Conquers All, an important source of future harmony is usually money. When Jack learns who he is, he not only comes into his own fortune but gives permission for Algernon to marry Cecily, who has her own money. In *Arms and the Man*, Raina's engagement to Bluntschli also has its practical side; besides being a professional soldier, Bluntschli, because of his father's death, is now a wealthy hotel owner.

We might ask at this point, what is the difference between this traditional comic resolution and the happy ending of a play like *A Raisin in the Sun?* The basic difference can be found in the view of life the author presents to the audience. A modern realistic play like *A Raisin in the Sun* is intended to give its audience a picture of life as it is. The ending of *A Raisin in the Sun* resolves conflicts within the Younger family, but the outside world is still a potential obstacle. In fact, Mama and the family must now face the greater challenge of racial bigotry hinted at by Lindner in his final line: "I sure hope you people know what you're doing." The happy ending of traditional comedy, on the other hand, offers the audience a picture of life as it should be. The resolution of conflict in comedy restores balance to the world of the play by reconciling the characters to prevailing social values, which are assumed to be just and beneficial to the individual.

The Resolution of Classical Tragedy

Today the word *tragedy* means disaster or catastrophe. A fatal air crash, an incurable disease, even a business failure, is called tragic. On the other hand, if a looming epidemic is avoided we say that tragedy was averted. In either case, we use the word to express how it feels to experience the clash of the elemental forces of being and nonbeing.

This clash is also present in classical tragedy. The protagonist **wants** to assert his being through action, **but** the forces of denial stand in the way and catastrophe follows. Classical tragedy, however, is not a celebration of the triumph of destruction. Rather, tragedy celebrates the revelation of a cosmic order in which the pendulum of human life swings between the poles of destruction and creation. This revelation comes about when catastrophe is survived and its meaning accepted. One kind of being may be destroyed, but another truer being is created. Comedy celebrates the renewal of life through the protagonist's victory, while in tragedy life is renewed through catastrophe.

As we have noticed, the happy ending of *A Raisin in the Sun* is not the same as a comic resolution. Likewise, the funereal ending of *Death of a Salesman* differs in important ways from the resolution of classical tragedy. In Sophocles' *Oedipus the King* and Shakespeare's *Hamlet,* the movement from recognition to final image involves the destruction and re-creation of a public, as well as a private, order. The discovery of Oedipus' guilt saves Thebes from annihilation and demonstrates to all that the gods mean what they say. The final moments of slaughter in *Hamlet* serve to remove a corrupt regime from the Danish throne. At the end of *Death of a Salesman,* by contrast, "the hard towers of the apartment buildings rise into sharp focus" over Willy's grave. The human world and the gods, if any, are indifferent to Willy's fate.

One of the purposes of the art of drama is to create order out of the chaos of life. At the same time, drama must stay in touch with the challenges of life or lose its vitality. This is why dramatic conventions are made, broken, and then remade. If audience expectations are never fulfilled, drama becomes incomprehensible; but if they are always fulfilled, it becomes boring and artificial. Skillful dramatists know when and how to upset conventions and usually do it with a specific purpose in mind. One of the ways to do this is to end the play in an unconventional way. Modern drama, especially, is full of unexpected endings. But classical dramatists, too, liked to vary the way they ended their plays. One of the most experimental classical dramatists was Euripides, whose use of the *deus ex machina* almost turned tragedy into comedy.

Deus ex machina

Deus ex machina refers to a practice in Greek theatre in which a cranelike device was used to lower actors onto the roof of the *skene* (scene building). These actors usually represented gods who appeared to be descending from the heavens. The god or gods usually arrived at the end of a play in which the conflict could not be resolved by mortals. They took matters into their own hands, resolved the situation, and restored harmony to the mortal world. In Script 6 we see how Euripides used the *deus ex machina* to wrap up the oft-told saga of the House of Atreus and even provide the long-suffering Electra with a husband.

The *deus ex machina* usually arrives at that moment in the play when we say, "It will take a miracle to get out of this." Such a moment occurs in the ending of Molière's *Tartuffe.* Since the play is a boy-meets-girl comedy, a conventional happy ending is in order. But the girl's father, Orgon, has foolishly given all his authority to the scoundrel Tartuffe, who now intends to send him to jail. But, miraculously, the King's Officer, who we thought had come for Orgon, has actually come for Tartuffe. Evidently the king has been keeping a keen eye on the problem:

Script 6
A Classical *Deus ex Machina* Scene from Euripides'
Electra (translated by Emily Townsend Vermeule).

Who's there? Orestes, his friend Pylades (a silent character), Electra,
  the body of Clytemnestra, whom they have just killed, a Chorus of
  Argive Peasant Women. The twin gods Castor and Pollux, known as
  the Dioscuri, appear on the roof of the *skene*. They were probably
  lowered onto the roof by a crane, or *machina*.
Setting. In front of the peasant dwelling where Electra has lived in exile.
Occasion. Orestes is told of his fate and of how the gods have tricked the
  Greeks into the Trojan War. Since the gods reveal everything about
  the past and the future, they resolve not only the tragic *situation,* but
  give the entire myth a happy ending.

[*The* DIOSCURI *appear on the roof, over the scene of mourning.*]
CHORUS: Whom do I see high over your house shining in radiance? Are
  they divinities or gods of the heavens? They are more than men in
  their moving. Why do they come so bright into the eyes of mortals?
DIOSCURI [CASTOR *speaking for both*]:
  O son of Agememnon, hear us: we call to you,
  the Twins, born with your mother, named the sons of Zeus . . .
  In Athens, in the hill of Ares . . .
  There you must also run the risk of trial for murder.
  But the voting-pebbles will be cast equal and save you,
  you shall not die by the verdict . . .

  Helen . . . never went to Troy.
  Zeus fashioned and dispatched a Helen-image there
  to Ilium so men might die in hate and blood.
  So. Let Pylades take Electra, girl and wife,
  and start his journey homeward . . .

The King soon recognized Tartuffe as one
Notorious by another name, who'd done
So many vicious crimes that one could fill
Ten volumes with them and be writing still.

And so Orgon is rescued and everything is returned—property, incriminating
private papers, family authority. Tartuffe is off to jail and Mariane can marry
Valère. Happy ending.

The *deus ex machina,* which celebrates an ideal, not a real, world, asks the
public to believe in miracles. This was natural enough for the Greek audience,
who had come to the theatre to honor the god Dionysus and to associate

themselves with one of his many miracles—the theatre. Even in Molière's day, many believed in the divinity, and most in the transcendent virtue, of King Louis XIV, who was often represented as an incarnation of the Greek god Apollo. Known as the Sun King, he was supposed to have been divinely inspired in all things. In *Tartuffe* the arrival of his officer to save the day was therefore in harmony with the popular mythology of the time.

Such beliefs are somewhat more difficult—but not impossible—to inspire in modern times. Audiences at performances of James M. Barrie's *Peter Pan* (1904) take on the role of *deus ex machina* themselves when Peter asks them to save the dying Tinkerbell by clapping their hands. The device never fails. The *deus ex machina* also survives in those dramatic endings which depend on the intervention of a superior or surprising force, such as the arrival of the U.S. cavalry or a last-minute pardon from the governor. Among modern dramatists, Bertolt Brecht makes ironic use of the *deus ex machina* in several of his plays.

Anticlimax

In linear plays, climax produces an explosion which shakes the world of the play. By contrast, the climactic event in mosaic drama might be said to produce an implosion—an inward bursting which has no important impact beyond a character's own situation. In Script 7, the ending of Chekhov's *The Sea Gull* is contrasted with that of Ibsen's *Hedda Gabler*. When Tesman opens the curtains in *Hedda Gabler*, every character in the play (except Lovborg, who is dead) is present in the dramatic space to witness the result of Hedda's horrifying deed. In *The Sea Gull,* only two of the seven characters present know that the offstage sound was a fatal gunshot. As the curtain falls, most of the people in the dramatic space go on with their card playing and socializing.

The anticlimactic ending has grown increasingly popular in modern drama as a means of expressing the isolation of the individual in an impersonal society. One of the most stunning uses of this device is in Eugene Ionesco's *The Chairs*. In this one-act play, an old man and woman face the end of their monotonous lives in a tower surrounded by water. The Old Man has invited many guests to the tower to hear a speech which will sum up the meaning of his life and pass his wisdom along to humanity. He has even hired a professional Orator to deliver the speech. When the guests begin to arrive we learn that they are invisible. But the Old Man and the Old Woman welcome them anyway, fetching chairs for each group of newcomers. By the time the Orator arrives, the stage is filled with chairs which, in turn, are filled with invisible people. The Old Man and Old Woman, having accomplished their life task, throw themselves out the window into the water. The Orator, a deaf-mute, then speaks:

ORATOR: He, mme, mm, mm. Ju, gou, hou, hou. Heu, heu, gu gou, gueue.

The curtain falls.

Script 7
Climax and Anticlimax in Realistic Drama

From Act IV of Henrik Ibsen's
Hedda Gabler (English version by Kari Borg).

Who's there? Tesman, Mrs. Elvsted, and Judge Brack. Hedda, Tesman's wife, is in the "inner room," which is hidden from the audience by a curtain.

Setting. The Tesman's living room and the adjoining inner room.

Occasion. Tesman and Mrs. Elvsted are excitedly making plans to work together on a valuable manuscript. Judge Brack, knowing this work will leave Hedda isolated, looks forward to having her in his power.

Situation. Hedda, who has lived her life underground, has other ideas.

[*A pistol shot is heard from the inner room.* TESMAN, MRS. ELVSTED, *and* JUDGE BRACK *jump to their feet.*]

TESMAN: She's playing with those pistols again! [*He throws open the curtains and goes in, followed by* MRS. ELVSTED. HEDDA *is stretched out on the sofa, lifeless. Confusion and cries.* BERTA *enters from the right, bewildered.*]

TESMAN [*screaming at* BRACK]: She's shot herself! Shot herself in the temple! Just think of it!

BRACK [*slumping into the chair*]: Good God—people don't do such things!

Curtain

Didactic Endings

A didactic ending is intended to teach by raising questions in playgoers' minds. Because of its strategic position at the gates of meaning, the ending of a play is sometimes used in this way by playwrights with highly personal or specific visions of human life. We have seen an example of a didactic ending in Euripides' *Electra* (Script 6), in which the use of *deus ex machina* serves two purposes. In the first place, it brings about the conventional tragic resolution of renewal through disaster. More important, however, it puts the audience in the position of questioning the very premise of conventional tragedy. In the final play of Aeschylus' trilogy, the *Oresteia*, Clytemnestra's death is seen from the perspective of the entire legend. In Euripides' *Electra* the opposite is true; the legend is seen in juxtaposition with the freshly butchered corpse of Clytemnestra. And what if, as Euripides suggests, the Trojan War *was* fought over an illusion? Are we simply using tragedy to glorify war and murder?

From Act IV of Anton Chekhov's
The Sea Gull (English version by Svetlana Caton-Noble).

Who's there? Irina Nikolayevna and her guests, five in number, including Dr. Dorn; also, a servant. Her son, Konstantin, is offstage,
in the next room.
Setting. A drawing room in the house on Irina's brother's estate.
Occasion. A social evening, to celebrate Irina's return to the country.
Situation. Konstantin feels unloved by both his mother and Nina, the
girl he loves.

[*Sound of a gunshot offstage. Everyone is startled.*]
DORN: Don't worry. [*Goes out door, returns immediately.*] Just as I
thought, a bottle of ether blew up. [*Sings casually.*] Once again,
I'm in your magic spell . . .
IRINA [*sitting at the table*]: How frightening! It made me remember—
[*Covers face.*] Everything went black—
DORN [*turning the pages of a magazine, to* TRIGORIN]: I saw an article
here—a letter from America I wanted to show you—[*Leads* TRI-
GORIN *downstage.*] I'm very interested in this—[*Lowers his
voice.*] Get Irina Nikolayevna away from here. The fact is, Kon-
stantin Gavrilovich has shot himself!
Curtain

This Euripidean fashion of asking the audience discomforting questions
is also prevalent in the modern theatre, especially in the plays of Ibsen, Shaw,
and Brecht.

In the final moments of Ibsen's *A Doll's House,* Nora tells her husband,
Torvald, that only a miracle could save their marriage and she no longer
believes in miracles. She leaves him alone on the stage, hoping. But no god
descends on a machine. Instead, the final stage direction reads, "The street
door is slammed shut downstairs." Because many people in the original
audience could not reconcile this ending with their own marriage ideals, the
play caused a scandal. A famous German actress of the time even threatened to
rewrite the ending. Ibsen, unprotected by copyright laws, preferred to do so
himself; *A Doll's House* was played, briefly, with Nora staying in the family.
But this ending did not work, because the original momentum of the entire
play was against it. Ibsen's original ending was restored and continued to ask
disquieting questions: Where does she go? What does she do? How can she just

leave her family this way? What happens to someone who decides to relearn her entire way of being?

At the end of Shaw's *Pygmalion*, Eliza Doolittle walks out on the man in her life, Henry Higgins. (The audience spends the entire play wondering when they will fall in love.) She does so because Higgins has made her into a doll. Like Nora, she is shown off at a ball and then rudely disillusioned by her man's indifference to her feelings. When she walks out on Higgins at the final curtain, the questions Ibsen asked in *A Doll's House* are asked once more. This ending gave Shaw the same kind of trouble it gave Ibsen, only more so. Disregarding Shaw's directions, the actor who created Henry Higgins threw a kiss to Eliza as the final curtain fell on the premiere performance (Shaw stormed out of the theatre). In *My Fair Lady*, the musical adaptation of *Pygmalion*, Eliza comes back at the last moment. The story of *Pygmalion*'s ending makes an interesting case study in how dramatic meaning is created through the interaction of the sometimes conflicting needs of author and audience.

In *Pygmalion*, Shaw withholds the happy ending the audience expects. In *The Threepenny Opera*, Shaw's admirer Bertolt Brecht gives us a happy ending we neither want nor wholly accept. The robber Macheath, who is thoroughly rotten, is about to be hanged, and he deserves it. However, because the actors do not want to take responsibility for such a deed, they decide to give us a happy ending instead. A *deus ex machina* arrives, in the form of a mounted messenger from the queen, and Macheath is not hanged, but lavishly rewarded for his life of crime. The outrageous artificiality of the ending causes us to question our belief in "mounted messengers" and our indifference to the social realities in which crime is rooted. "Never be too eager to combat injustice," advises one character before the final song. This sounds both sensible and wrong! Where do we stand? The ending requires the audience to face the reality of its own position on social injustice.

Brecht also used a kind of reverse *deus ex machina* in his play *The Good Woman of Setzuan*. In the beginning of the play, the gods come to earth in search of a good person. What they discover is that the world as it is makes it impossible for people to be good to themselves or to others. Seeing no way to resolve the situation, they fly away at the end of the play, leaving the mortals with the problem. "Ladies and gentlemen, don't be angry," says the Epilogue. "We're disappointed, too. . . . We see the curtain closed, the plot unended. In your opinion, then, what's to be done?" By placing the audience in the position of gods, Brecht hopes to teach us to think for ourselves rather than rely on the *deus ex machina* of conventional ideals.

In the theatre the end of the play is usually followed by a curtain call. In this long-standing ritual, actors and audience acknowledge one another's role in the creation of the theatre event. The imaginary world is left behind and all join together in the real world. Printed drama cannot, of course, contain a curtain call, although many endings, such as the epilogues of Shakespeare, do seem to reach out from the page as if to embrace the reader.

As readers, however, we reenter the real world alone. But, although we don't have actors to help us, we do have one advantage that is not available in live performance. We can replay the ending immediately and as often as we like. We can review the feelings and ideas which culminate there simply by thumbing through the pages of the script. We can consider important questions at our own pace. Which conflicts are resolved and which are projected into the future? Which characters emerge into the light of discovery and which remain in shadows? What depth or breadth of recognition takes place? And, finally, what vision of human life does the play offer?

Play Reader's Checklist

We all think we know what a play is, but no one has ever succeeded in defining it. A novel or a poem is neither more nor less than the words it consists of, but a script is obviously less than a play, while a production is obviously more. So how do we locate its limits? Is it like a chemical substance which can never be isolated, existing only in combination with other substances?
—from *How To Read a Play,* by Ronald Hayman

More than a script, the play is created from images of action in the reader's imagination. And, although the play may be, in a sense, less than a production, the skillful reader will always remain aware of the dimension of performance. If a play is the result of a chemical reaction between reader and script, the following questions may function as catalysts:

- *What kind of play is it?*
  Maybe you can't tell a book by its cover, but you can tell a lot about a play by its title page and cast of characters. First of all, is the play classical or modern? If it was written before the late 1900s, chances are you can apply the guidelines for classical drama, including the linear plot and the comic or tragic resolution. If it is a modern play, it is a good idea to familiarize yourself first of all with the setting by reading introductory stage directions. Then get as much background as you can from the list of characters. By this time you may be ready to make some educated guesses about what kind of action to expect. Whether your guesses are right or wrong, they will give you a beginning framework for your study of the play.

- *What is the conflict?*
  Get in touch with tension-producing conflict and watch where it goes. Find out who has the most persistent purpose, what the obstacles are, and what this character does about it. If you can't answer these questions intuitively, try using one of the formulas for conflict or character.

- *How is the story told?*
  Is there a steady buildup of tension which explodes in a climax? Or are there random variations on a theme which accumulate into a composite image?

- *Are there subplots and subprotagonists?*
  This is an important question especially in the drama of Shakespeare.

- *Is there a truth-facing scene?*
  Is the truth faced privately or in the presence of other characters? What impact does this moment have on the world of the play?

- *What vision of the future does the play project?*
  Are things changed or unchanged? Is the final image that of an ideal or a real world? What values seem to govern this world? How do you relate to these values and this vision of the future? How do you imagine an audience of your peers would respond?

Part Three

Classical Drama
Images of Action
Artfully Assembled
for a Conventionalized
Theatre Event

9 ❦ Introduction to Classical Drama

> *Playgoers, I bid you welcome. The theatre is a temple, and we are here to worship the gods of comedy and tragedy.*
> —*A Funny Thing Happened on the Way to the Forum* (Shevelove, Gelbart, and Sondheim)

*T*he term *classical drama* is used in several different ways. In the narrowest sense, it means the drama of ancient Greece and Rome. In a broader sense, it can refer to all drama which is not modern. In Part Three we look at the three kinds of classical drama the beginning reader is most likely to encounter: Greek tragedy, Shakespearean drama, and the comedy of manners of the seventeenth and eighteenth centuries.

Modern scripts, most of which are prepared for publication by their authors, usually supply the reader with a great deal of information in stage directions and even, in the case of Bernard Shaw, fully developed prefaces. Classical scripts, on the other hand, were not written with a reader in mind. The classical dramatist's main concern was to create raw material for performance, and the function of the script was simply to enable the actor to deliver the play to the audience. We can read a classical script with greater understanding, then, if we know something about the kind of theatre event it was intended for. In this introductory chapter, we survey the general nature of the theatre event, the several functions of dialogue, important aspects of character, and the underlying importance of convention in classical drama.

The Classical Spirit

In the old television show "Star Trek," Captain Kirk and his fellow officers travel through space in the form of light. When beamed aboard the starship *Enterprise* after the latest interplanetary adventure, their bodies are fragmented into particles of light and then magically reassembled in the safety of the spacecraft. This is, for the most part, how the modern actor makes entrances and exits—as if borne on a beam of light. When the television is switched on or when the movie fades in, the actor appears. In the theatre, house lights dim, acting areas fade up—there is the actor. As the lights fade out, the actor disappears and the show is over.

The classical actor's electricity, on the other hand, came from within. He had to create the theatre event armed only with the author's words and the magic of his physical presence, augmented by costume, wig, or mask. This actor learned his craft in the school of hard knocks, playing in makeshift circumstances before demanding audiences, often outdoors at the mercy of sun and shower. He was sometimes not paid until the end of the performance—if the audience liked the show. A permanent theatre building was not something to be taken for granted. It was a coveted award for the few who survived grueling apprenticeships "on the road."

The most vivid images we have of the classical actor are found in the works of Shakespeare. In *Hamlet* (Script 8), for instance, a company of traveling players find themselves in Elsinore Castle after a hard day's journey. Before they have had time to unpack, their patron, a stagestruck young prince, wants to hear "a passionate speech." "What speech, my good lord?" asks the lead actor. This First Player knows scores of plays by heart. It is his professional duty to have a full menu of dramatic fare ready at all times for his public. As the scene proceeds, he gives a solo performance which so impresses the prince that he orders up a complete play, with some additional dialogue of his own, for the next evening's entertainment—all in a day's work for the First Player and his company.

In this scene and others, Shakespeare offers us images of traveling players giving private shows in informal circumstances. Of course, classical actors also played in permanent theatres, and most of the classical drama we read was written for these theatres. But even the most highly developed classical stages—the Theatre of Dionysus in Athens, Shakespeare's Globe, and the seventeenth-century Parisian theatres of Molière—housed performances which were, in spirit, simply amplifications and extensions of the touring show. The primary function of these theatres was to enhance the presence of the actor in a permanent structure, where the audience could assemble in reasonable comfort.

The Classical Theatre Event

In ancient Greece, sea, sky, hills, and the unseen world of the gods provided a permanent cosmic context for performances which were both religious celebration and Olympics-style competition. The audience sat in a fan-shaped, hillside amphitheater surrounding a large circular area. Running along the far side of the circle, opposite the seating area, was a permanent structure from which the impressively masked and costumed actors made their entrances. Every Greek play we have was written for this kind of theatre.

The late sixteenth-century theatres of Shakespeare and his contemporaries mark an interesting transition from outdoor to indoor theatre. Part roofed and part open, they were still in contact with nature but also contained the beginnings of the artificial environment into which drama was to move. Shakespeare's scripts reflect his stage—elaborate, flexible, and capable of a

Script 8

From Act II, scene 2 of Shakespeare's
Hamlet.

Who's there? Hamlet, Polonius, Rosencrantz, Guildenstern, Players
Setting. A room in Elsinore Castle.
Occasion. Hamlet greets his old friends, the Players, who have come to
entertain the court.

[*Enter four or five* PLAYERS.]
HAMLET: You are welcome, masters, welcome all.—I am glad to see thee
well—Welcome, good friends.—O, my old friend! Why, thy face
is valanc'd since I saw thee last. Com'st thou to beard me in Denmark?—What, my young lady and mistress? By'r lady, your Lady-
ship is nearer to heaven than when I saw you last by the altitude of a
chopine. Pray God your voice, like a piece of uncurrent gold, be not
crack'd within the ring.—Masters, you are all welcome. We'll e'en
to't like French falconers, fly at anything we see. We'll have a speech
straight. Come, give us a taste of your quality. Come, a passionate
speech.
FIRST PLAYER: What speech, my good lord?

Vocabulary
Valanc'd: One of the actors has grown a beard.
Beard me: Take me by the beard to gain an advantage; also, provide me
with a disguise.
My young lady: The boy actor who played the women's parts.
Chopine: Platform shoes worn by the boy actor.
Crack'd within the ring: If the boy actor's voice has changed, he can no
longer play female roles.

broad range of dramatic effects. The audience was wrapped three-quarters of
the way around the actors in three vertically stacked seating levels as well as in
ground floor standing room. This arrangement assured the feeling of the
actor-audience unity which characterizes classical drama. Shakespeare made
continual use of this potential for direct audience contact in prologues, epilogues, asides, and soliloquies.

In the seventeenth and eighteenth centuries the theatre moved completely
indoors, but actors and audience still maintained contact and shared a sense of
the communal nature of dramatic performance. Although somewhat more
separated than in Greek and Shakespearean theatres, both auditorium and
stage were lit by candles, and the actors made plentiful use of that part of the
stage which was closest to the audience.

✿ *The Rough Road of Classical Theatre*

The first actor, Thespis, packed his shows in a cart and toured rural Greece. Only when his fame reached the ears of Peisistratus, King of Athens, was a permanent outdoor theatre erected for the Thespian event. The actors who built the Globe Theatre in London were successful traveling performers who had for years set up their shows in dining halls and inn yards. Molière spent the first decades of his actor's life on tour in the French provinces. When Louis XIV gave him patronage and space in Paris, he was still expected to act in converted tennis courts, the Louvre, the royal palace at Versailles, or, at one sticky moment, in a theatre which was about to be torn down by royal decree (Louis XIV was a generous, but forgetful, patron of the arts).

In modern drama, that crucible of action we call dramatic space is defined by the particular physical, visual, aural, and movement requirements of each script. But in classical drama, dramatic space is conditioned by the permanent features of the theatre structure. Dramatic action is part character behavior and part interplay with the audience. And, of paramount importance to the reader, these conditions are not spelled out in stage directions. They were assumed by the author to be understood by anyone who read his script. As readers of classical drama, then, we will find our way more easily if we can connect with the characters and imagine dramatic space in terms of the kind of theatre event implicit in the script.

To Hear a Play

The reader of classical drama enters a world in which dialogue plays a larger role than in most modern drama. When Hamlet commands the First Player to perform he says, "We'll have a speech." "We hear it," says the duke in Shakespeare's *A Midsummer Night's Dream,* as he chooses the play for his wedding celebration. The prologue to Shakespeare's *Henry V* asks the audience "gently to hear, kindly to judge, our play." This does not mean that classical performances were without visual interest—far from it. But it does mean that the foundation of this drama is in the dialogue. Its basic appeal is to the mind's ear.

Classical dialogue performs many functions. For one, it is the vehicle through which thoughts and feelings are clearly, completely, and effectively expressed. Modern dialogue tends to imitate the way people actually talk. But classical dialogue is written the way people *would* talk, if they were as articulate as the author. (One modern dramatist who wrote dialogue in the classical manner is Bernard Shaw.) For instance, we may know what it feels like to wait for a lover's message. But how many of us could express this feeling as vividly as Shakespeare's Juliet as she waits for the Nurse to return with words from Romeo:

> The clock struck nine when I did send the nurse;
> In half an hour she promised to return. . . .
> Now is the sun upon the highmost hill
> Of this day's journey, and from nine to twelve
> Is three long hours: yet she is not come.
> Had she affections and warm youthful blood,
> She would be as swift in motion as a ball;
> My words would bandy her to my sweet love
> And his to me.
> But old folks, many feign as they were dead—
> Unwieldy, slow, heavy, and pale as lead.

A fourteen-year-old girl would probably not talk this eloquently in reality. But she could certainly feel this deeply, and Shakespeare's goal was not to create real talk, but to express strong feeling.

In classical drama the evocation of setting and atmosphere, found in stage directions in modern scripts, is done mainly through dialogue. Macbeth contemplates nightfall with these words:

> Light thickens; and the crow
> Makes wing to the rooky wood:
> Good things of day begin to droop and drowse;
> Whiles night's black agents to their preys do rouse.

And Oberon, in *A Midsummer Night's Dream,* conveys the feeling of the sun rising over the sea (Neptune):

> I with the Morning's love have oft made sport,
> And, like a forester, the groves may tread
> Even till the eastern gate, all fiery red,
> Opening on Neptune, with fair blessed beams
> Turns into yellow gold his salt green streams.

In a theatre without electric light, such language charged the audience's imagination directly with the feeling, rather than the look, of night and day.

Another important function of classical dialogue is to communicate details of occasion (what are they doing?) and situation (what's wrong?). In Act I of *Hamlet,* while Horatio waits for the Ghost to appear, he briefs Marcellus and Bernardo on recent Danish military and political history. He recognizes that the soldiers may already know the story, but since the audience does not, he gives a full account of the chain of events which have led up to the activities of the present moment. The new King of Denmark is getting ready for a possible invasion by Norwegian forces seeking to gain back land which they lost to the former king, old Hamlet. What's more, these forces are led by the son of the man old Hamlet killed in battle. Named for his father, young Fortinbras may have revenge on his mind. This clarification of an aspect of the opening occasion in *Hamlet* foreshadows the Ghost's demand for revenge, which becomes the heart of the situation.

In addition to fully expressing thoughts and feelings and supplying detailed background, classical dialogue often provides the reader with a moral or philosophical perspective from which to view the action. The scholar Horatio ends his lecture on Danish politics by comparing the atmosphere at Elsinore to that of Rome before the fall of Julius Caesar, placing the action of the play in the context of recurrent cycles of world history.

In Sophocles' *Oedipus the King,* the Chorus of Theban Elders reflects on the nature of kingship:

> The tyrant drinks his cup of pride
> And climbs beyond our sight,
> Then, blazing like an evil star
> Falls into endless night.
> Yet he who for the people's good
> Works humbly in his power
> Builds high above the city walls
> A strong enduring tower.

These thoughts on kingly behavior offer us several ways of thinking about Oedipus without directing our judgment to any particular conclusion.

In many comedies of manners, a philosophical character is included in the cast. Cléante, in Molière's *Tartuffe,* articulates an ideal of moderation by which to measure the characters' behavior:

> There's true and false in piety, as in bravery,
> And just as those whose courage shines the most
> In battle, are least inclined to boast,
> So those whose hearts are truly pure and lowly
> Don't make a flashy show of being holy.

A drama of contradictions, *Hamlet* contains contradictory moral precepts uttered by contrasting characters:

POLONIUS: This above all: to thine own self be true . . .

HAMLET: Assume a virtue if you have it not . . .

Note that moral and philosophical generalizations in classical dialogue do not necessarily convey the meaning of the play. Rather, they suggest possibly meaningful implications of the action. Meaning, in drama, is a dynamic process and cannot be reduced to any specific lines of dialogue.

Character in Classical Drama

In most drama written for the modern theatre, and in virtually all mass media drama, the characters are usually meant to be recognizable and autonomous individuals—"real people." Care is taken, both in writing and acting, to create behavior which is "in character" and to avoid that which is "out of character." Modern audiences look for characters whose behavior is both consistent and familiar, and modern producers try to supply them.

Classical drama does not always follow these rules. First of all, characters in classical plays tend to represent typical rather than individual behavior. Actors in Greek tragedy wore masks which symbolized the type of character they were protraying: the powerful king, the young prince, the daughter in mourning, the messenger, and so on. Many Shakespearean characters were handed down from medieval dramatic types. Iago, in *Othello,* is a descendant of Vice, a character who in medieval drama represents hellish evil unleashed on earth. Macbeth resembles the popular biblical character Herod, who slaughtered innocent babes. In *Henry IV, Parts One and Two,* and *Henry V,* Prince Hal symbolizes the "new man" who emerges from the Christian process of Redemption. As the brooding and alienated avenger, Hamlet is one example of a very popular Elizabethan character type. The names of many comedy-of-manners' characters indicate their type immediately: Sir Fopling Flutter, Lady Sneerwell, Lydia Languish, and Orgon (suggesting pridefulness in French).

The reader can best approach these type characters of classical drama by making empathic and imaginative connection with their behavior, bearing in mind that it may seem more general and externalized than the behavior of characters in modern drama. Some commentators claim the "real people" method of characterization is inherently superior, while others assert that classical characters, having stood the test of time, are more vital and deserving of our study. Fortunately, we are not forced to choose between these two approaches. We can enjoy both kinds of character, just as we enjoy the many kinds of humanity we find in the real world.

A second important aspect of character in classical drama is what John Dexter, Director of the Royal Shakespeare Company, calls choric behavior, that is, behavior which is like that of a chorus, or model audience. Such "characters" as the Chorus in *Romeo and Juliet* often speak to the audience from outside the action. But choric behavior is not confined to choruses and prologues. Any character in classical drama may function, from time to time, as an audience to the action. This does not, however, change the reader's approach to classical character. Choric behavior simply has different objectives than behavior that is "in character." Typical choric objectives are to warm up the audience, to inform, to conspire, to reflect on the action, and to encourage applause.

Convention in Classical Drama

When everyone agrees on a particular way of doing things, it is a *convention*. Although we moderns place a high value on innovation, classical cultures valued the idea of doing certain things in the same way every time. By adhering to conventions, they were able to preserve their social values and ideals and provide the individual with a sense of continuity in a mysterious and unpredictable universe. Along with religion, drama was one of those institutions in which convention was valued. Playwrights, actors, and audiences liked to agree beforehand on where they were going and on a certain set of rules for getting there. Because new rules and goals did not have to be invented for each theatre event, more attention could be devoted to interesting variations and nuances in dramatic content. Conventions in classical drama assured continuity and efficiency for audiences and artists alike.

Dramatic conventions are of two kinds: those having to do with the theatre event and those associated with dramatic structure. We have already briefly surveyed the theatres which produced Greek tragedy, Shakespearean drama, and the comedy of manners. Each of these playhouses had its own performance conventions which are reflected in the scripts of that period and do not apply to the scripts of any other period. On the other hand, many elements of dramatic structure survive from era to era. Conflict and recognition are key aspects of all classical drama. Most classical characters, as mentioned previously, are based on conventional types and may demonstrate choric behavior. And some of the basic conventions of tragedy and comedy reappear in all classical periods. To the contemporary reader, classical dramatic conventions offer unity and efficiency, the same advantages they offered to those who invented them. Once we understand the conventions of a particular theatre, we can apply them to all plays written for that theatre. And once we understand certain conventions of dramatic structure, we can apply them to all classical, and much modern, drama.

10 ❦ Greek Tragedy

AESCHYLUS: Euripides, tell me:
What do you consider the chief duty of a
poet?
EURIPIDES: To speak truth for the improvement
of the city.
—Aristophanes' *The Frogs*, translated by Dudley Fitts

*T*he further back we move in the history of drama, the greater is the presence of the natural universe in the theatre event. Neoclassical playhouses were completely enclosed structures. Shakespeare's Globe was partly open to the elements. The Greek Theatre of Dionysus was installed in a hillside and fully open to sun and sky. This changing relationship to nature is reflected in drama. The comedy of manners is mostly about social relationships. Shakespearean drama is full of evocations of the natural world and questions about humanity's place in it. The Greeks believed in the coexistence of the natural and supernatural worlds, and the dramatic performances of the fifth century B.C. took place, to their minds, in full view of the gods.

The Greeks honored their gods with two kinds of dramatic performance, each in a separate season—tragedy in the spring and comedy in the winter. Although he was a writer of comedies, Aristophanes occasionally included his tragedy-writing colleagues in his cast of characters. In *The Frogs*, first performed in 405 B.C., Aristophanes introduces us to Aeschylus, Sophocles, and Euripides, the three tragic dramatists whose work survives today. In the play, Dionysus, the god in whose honor tragedy was performed, journeys to the underworld in the hope of reviving Euripides, whose recent death has left the theatre without a major tragic poet (as playwrights were then called). When the god arrives, he is asked to judge a debate on the subject of tragedy between Euripides and his older rival, Aeschylus. Compared with Aeschylus' traditional stance, Euripides' approach to drama sounds almost like modern realism. Aeschylus defends his high-sounding, and sometimes obscure, dialogue by pointing out that it is consistent with the visual style of "our actor-demigods" (Greek actors did, in fact, look godlike in their exaggerated costumes and stylized masks). Although they clash violently about tragic style and subject matter, both tragedians agree that the poet's chief duty is "to speak truth for the improvement of the city."

We learn several things about Greek tragedy from *The Frogs*. For one thing, we see that tragedy must have been a subject which Aristophanes'

audience knew something about. For another, we get a kind of capsule summary of the three dramatists. Aeschylus was the oldest, the conservative
"father of tragedy." Euripides was the young rebel, who drew sharp satirical
fire from the neoconservative Aristophanes in more than one comedy. And in
the middle, providing the center of balance, was Sophocles, veteran of thirty
years of competition in the Festival of Dionysus and author of what has
become the best-known Greek tragedy, *Oedipus the King*.

The Festival of Dionysus

While we moderns look to the future as an ideal time to come, the Greeks
viewed the past as a golden age, in which men and gods lived the answers to
universal questions. Myths were told and retold about this ideal time that used
to be. During a dramatic performance at the Festival of Dionysus, the audience
could imagine they were back in ancient times witnessing these myths with
their own eyes.

The performance of tragedy at the Festival of Dionysus, or City Dionysia,
began in 554 B.C. The performances, held in Athens' Theatre of Dionysus, were
part religious ritual, part popular entertainment, and part contest in which
tragic poets competed for prizes, just as athletes did in the Olympics. All work
stopped for two or three weeks in the spring, and everybody joined the
celebration in honor of Dionysus, god of wine, fertility, and rebirth. Atten-
dance was both an exciting diversion and a civic obligation, and if a playgoer
couldn't afford a ticket, it was paid for by the city. Since the event attracted
many foreign visitors, civic pride was everywhere on display. There was no
higher honor in Athens than to win first prize for the best production, which,
according to the rules, meant three tragedies (a *trilogy*) and a short afterpiece,
a *satyr play*.

The Greek tragedians took it for granted that their audiences already knew
the stories of the plays they came to see. The art of the tragic poet was not in
presenting new material but in finding fresh truths in the ancient myths. The
two most popular myths seem to have been those dealing with the royal houses
of Atreus and Thebes. Of the thirty-three Greek tragedies which survive,
fifteen are about the House of Atreus, including the three plays of Aeschylus'
Oresteia, the only surviving example of the trilogy format in which the plays
were performed. Among their House of Atreus plays, Sophocles and Euripides
each included an *Electra*, which tells the same story as the second play of the
Oresteia. Three of the five surviving Theban plays are by Sophocles. Although
sometimes printed together, these three do not constitute a trilogy since they
were performed at different festivals: *Antigone* in 441 B.C.; *Oedipus the King*
(also known as *Oedipus Rex, King Oedipus,* or *Oedipus Tyrannos*) in 430
B.C.; and *Oedipus at Colonus* (or *Oedipus Coloneus*) in 406 B.C. Sophocles
was the all-time City Dionysia champion, winning twenty-four first prizes and
six second prizes in thirty years of competition.

Prizes at the City Dionysia were given for drama in performance, and the scripts that have survived contain only the original dialogue. Stage directions, by and large, are the work of translators and editors who must make inferences about the plays from the small stock of knowledge of Greek performance. The nature of these inferences vary according to the purposes and assumptions of the translators, most of whom are primarily concerned with the difficult task of rendering an ancient language into English that is both intelligible and faithful. Some translations are made from the point of view of the Greek theatre, while some are adapted to modern threatre practice. Still others may treat the play as a poem, with no reference at all to performance. Whatever the translator's point of view, we can imagine dramatic space and audience response more vividly if we bear in mind the fundamentals of the Dionysian theatre event. Because the Festival of Dionysus was supposed to embody the eternal truths of Greek culture, these fundamentals were subject to very little change. Holding a picture of them in our mind's eye can help us read any Greek drama—the comedies of Aristophanes, as well as the tragedies of Aeschylus, Sophocles, and Euripides.

The Theatre of Dionysus

Script 9 contains a passage from Sophocles' *Oedipus the King*. If we imagine a god's-eye view of this scene in performance at the Theatre of Dionysus, we see something like the following. Twenty thousand spectators are seated on wooden or stone seats on a hillside, which is wrapped around three sides of a circular area forty feet in diameter—the *orchestra*, or "dancing place." In this circle are the twelve members of the chorus who, for this performance, represent the elders of Thebes, the oldest and most respected members of the community. Along the far side of the orchestra is a permanent two- or three-story structure, the *skene*, from which the actors make their entrances. As is often the case, this structure represents the king's palace. Along the front of the *skene* there is probably a platform about four feet high. On this platform are the two actors playing Oedipus and Teiresias. They look almost super-human in their large, grotesque masks and high wigs, stiff, padded robes, and boots with elevated soles.

This performance of *Oedipus the King* follows the same pattern as all Greek tragedy. Dialogue between the characters (*episodes*) alternates with the dialogue of the chorus (*odes*) in a rhythm of action and response. The actors come and go through the doors of the *skene,* while the chorus remains in the orchestra to witness and sometimes participate in the episodes and to guide the audience's reaction in the odes.

In the earliest Greek tragedy, the episodes featured only one character interacting with the chorus or chorus leader. Later, the potential for conflict was increased by adding a second and third actor. Although the cast of a Greek tragedy may include more than three characters, their entrances and exits are arranged so that all parts can be played by three actors, with a change of

Script 9
From Sophocles'
King Oedipus (English version by John Lewin).

Who's there? Oedipus, Teiresias, and the Chorus of Theban Elders.
Setting. Thebes, in front of the palace of King Oedipus.
Occasion. Oedipus, investigating the murder of the former king, is questioning the prophet Teiresias.
Situation. Although it is inconceivable to Oedipus, he himself is the culprit.

TEIRESIAS: You have no friend in Thebes, for you are its curse.
OEDIPUS: You think you can say that, and escape punishment?
TEIRESIAS: Oedipus, *I* do not need to escape the truth.
OEDIPUS: Who prompted you in this? It was not the god!
TEIRESIAS: You did, by making me speak against my will.
OEDIPUS: Say it more clearly. Let there be no mistake.
TEIRESIAS: You seek the king's murderer. It is you.
OEDIPUS: You will regret those words.
TEIRESIAS: I have more food for your rage, since you like to gorge it.
OEDIPUS: Speak on; you have hanged yourself twice already.
TEIRESIAS: Your union with the person you love most is one of foulest shame.
OEDIPUS: Will you go on with this?
TEIRESIAS: The truth will go on without me.
OEDIPUS: It *must* do so, for you have never known it. Your mind and heart are darker than your eyes.
TEIRESIAS: I pity you, Oedipus, for all these things will be said of you.
OEDIPUS: You pity me! You, groping in darkness. What can you do to a man who sees the sun?
TEIRESIAS: There is nothing for me to do. What will be done will be done by Apollo.
OEDIPUS: Wait. Was it Creon who told you to say this?
TEIRESIAS: Your enemy is not Creon, but yourself.

masks. All three may be present and even speak in one episode, but the typical dramatic segment is the kind of one-on-one struggle we find in Script 9. In this scene, King Oedipus, investigating a murder, has just heard himself accused of the crime by the blind prophet, Teiresias. The tension of rapid back-and-forth dialogue is released in Oedipus' angry counter accusation against not only Teiresias, but Creon, Oedipus' second in command. Of great importance is the fact that this frightening display of deadly threat and recrimination between king and prophet takes place in public, in the presence of the Elders.

The Chorus

Since the Greek audience was long accustomed to the action-reaction rhythm of their drama, they knew that a choral ode would be heard when the Oedipus-Teiresias episode was finished. The audience can therefore be imagined as anticipating choral response to the shocking events of the drama. Modern readers are sometimes tempted to skip choral passages, but to the Greek audience the odes were a crucial part of the play. The chorus represent the Theban Elders, who, in the fictional world of the play, are deeply concerned with the fate of their city. They also perform the priestly function of speaking for and to the gods in the real world of the audience. Aristophanes expressed the Greek perception of the chorus when he wrote:

> There is no function more noble than that
> > of the god-touched Chorus
> Teaching the City in Song.

This tradition of spiritual teaching in Greek tragedy is centered in the choral odes. The chorus are partly encircled by the audience to provide maximum contact in those moments when the drama "speaks truth for the improvement of the city."

For the reader, this means that, after they have entered, the chorus are a part of dramatic space during the episodes and the center of the theatre event when alone with the audience during the odes. When they are silent, their reactions are anticipated. When they speak, we connect directly with their feelings and thoughts. Anticipating and empathizing with the reactions of the chorus heightens our own response awareness and highlights the importance of response itself as an element of drama.

Who are the chorus and what are they doing? Although some translators assign the dialogue of choral odes variously between half-choruses or among chorus leaders (sometimes called *choragos* or *choryphaios*), or divide the lines according to poetic structure (for example, *strophe* and *antistrophe*), little is known about how the chorus actually performed. In most scripts, they enter the orchestra after the first episode, or prologue. This entrance is called the *parodos,* and must have made an important rhythmic and visual contribution to the performance. It is difficult to believe that they did not sing and dance, although to what kind of music and choreography we cannot say. The best guess is that flutes and drums, at least, accompanied the chorus and maybe even the actors. Readers may want to imagine their own choreography when they see "Enter the Chorus" in a Greek script.

While the physical activities of the choral members will remain somewhat shadowy, we can learn a lot from the script about who they are and how they think and feel. Each Greek chorus has a separate identity, usually given in the cast of characters. In the *Oresteia* the chorus represents, in turn, the elders of Argos, foreign serving women, and a group of demigods, the Furies. Sophocles' choruses include two of Theban elders and two of sailors. In the nineteen dramas of Euripides, the chorus may be anything from Argive peasant women to Bacchae, the frenzied followers of Dionysus.

Choruses also display a variety of behavior. Aeschylus' choruses tend to be morally committed and directly involved in the action. In his *Eumenides*, the third play of the *Oresteia*, the Chorus of Furies are seeking revenge against Orestes for having murdered his mother, Clytemnestra. When the goddess Athena decides that Orestes should be forgiven, the Furies howl with outrage (in a translation which handles them as a single character):

> That they should treat me so!
> I, the mind of the past, to be driven under the ground
> out cast, like dirt!
> The wind I breathe is fury and utter hate.

A typical Sophoclean chorus is also morally committed, but sometimes detached in regard to specific issues. When the evidence that Oedipus is a murderer seems to be mounting, the Chorus of Theban Elders focuses on maintaining its own spiritual poise:

> Be it said of me, whatever else
> I earn of blame or praise:
> "He walked the way of righteousness
> Ordained in ancient days."

With the important exception of the Bacchae, Euripides' choruses are often uncommitted and uninvolved, providing ironic comment as counterpoint to the action. As his Electra and Orestes prepare to kill their mother and her lover, the Chorus of Argive Peasant Women seem to ignore the action completely in their ode:

> The ancient tale is told in Argos
> still—how a magic lamb
> from its mother gay on the hills
> Pan stole, Pan of the wild
> beasts, kind watcher, Pan
> who breathes music to his jointed reed . . .

But, as the ode continues, the stolen lamb is developed into a symbol of violated innocence which can be applied to every stage of the tragic history of the House of Atreus, now about to end. The Chorus of Argive Peasant Women, although seemingly indifferent, bring their own kind of timeless folk wisdom to bear on the action of the play. If we grant the chorus the same individuality as we do the characters, Greek tragedy will play all the more vividly in our imaginations.

The twelve- to fifteen-member chorus occupies a large share of the dramatic space during the episodes, and it is the center of the theatre event during the odes. Its presence, together with the typical outdoor public settings of the plays—the palaces, temples, tombs, and sacred groves represented by the *skene*—is a constant reminder that the action of Greek tragedy takes place not only in full public view but in the sight of the gods. The chorus watching the actors can be imagined as a mirror image of the audience watching the performance. The audience, chorus, and actors together can then be imagined as representing the world of mortals, which was itself a spectacle for the gods. The public and cosmic events which are the subject of Greek tragedy are dramatic counterparts of the public and cosmic event which was the Festival of Dionysus.

Conflict and Recognition

Greek tragedy, as we have seen, follows a regular pattern of action and response. An episode of conflict is followed by the chorus' reaction in an ode, followed by another episode of conflict. The typical Greek tragedy has six episodes, including the prologue; and six odes, including the *parodos* (entrance of the chorus) and *exodos* (exit of the chorus). Sometimes the entire dénouement, including the final episode and ode, is the *exodos*. But, whatever labels are used in the script, the fundamental rhythm of action and response is always followed.

Every episode contains a clear conflict, usually between two characters, but sometimes between a character and the chorus or chorus leader. A third character may, on occasion, be included in the episode, either as part of the conflict or as an observer. A silent character may also be present. The characters' objectives are usually stark and simple. In *Oedipus the King,* Oedipus wants to find the murderer; in the various *Electra* plays, Electra and Orestes want to avenge their father's murder; King Creon, in Sophocles' *Antigone,* wants to restore civic order by refusing burial to the defeated rebel leader.

At first, the obstacles appear to be human. The protagonist is opposed by an *antagonist*. Teiresias and Creon seem to stand in Oedipus' way; Electra's mother, murderess of Electra's father, keeps her prisoner and sends her brother, Orestes, into exile; Antigone, the rebel leader's sister, defies the king's order and buries her brother. As the situation unfolds, however, a greater-than-human obstacle comes into play. The tragic protagonist finds that he is up against cosmic forces: the god Apollo has decreed from the beginning that Oedipus would murder his father; after Electra and Orestes joyfully collaborate in revenge, the Furies appear and drive Orestes again into exile; Creon's edict against burial, setting civic law over religious tradition, backfires as he is overtaken by political and domestic disaster.

The tragic conflict, then, is finally revealed as a clash between mortal striving and a mysterious force in the universe which opposes such striving. Sometimes it is said that Greek tragedy is about man against the gods, and it is true that a god may sometimes be the agent of negative forces, as is Apollo in

Oedipus the King. But a god may also take the side of mortals, as Apollo does in *The Libation Bearers,* or may be, like Athena in the *Eumenides,* the agent of reconciliation. The conflict in Greek tragedy reveals forces to which both mortals and gods are subject.

Recognition in Greek tragedy takes place at human and cosmic levels. At the human level, one character discovers the true identity of another. A famous moment of recognition occurs in the *Electra* plays. Electra has been longing for her brother Orestes' return every day of the many years he has been gone. When he returns he is at first in disguise but then proves his identity. When she realizes who he is, her whole life situation is reversed. In Sophocles' version of the story, another recognition occurs when Clytemnestra comes out of the palace to view what she has been told is the body of Orestes. When she sees the face of the corpse, she recognizes, not Orestes, but her lover, Aegisthus. At that moment, she realizes that Orestes has returned and the process of revenge has already begun. Whereas recognition brought Electra a positive reversal, it brings Clytemnestra a negative one.

Recognition at the cosmic level is tied in with the final resolution of the conflict between human striving and the forces of denial. The Greeks believed in a universal principle which reconciled the forces of creation and destruction. They called it *Moira,* translated variously as Fate, or Necessity. To the modern mind, Necessity is an unfamiliar idea. We believe, instead, in progress—the idea that we can assert ourselves unconditionally and that, some day in the future, we will triumph once and for all over the forces of denial. The fascination in reading Greek tragedy, however, is in reading it as if we believed that our being cannot be asserted unconditionally, and that we occupy a small place in an immense universe in which all things, even the immortal gods, are subject to the one force, Necessity. It is the recognition of Necessity, in one form or another, that finally resolves the conflict in Greek tragedy.

Plot and Character

The plot of Greek tragedy exists at two levels: the individual play and the trilogy. The plots of individual plays are linear and move directly and logically from conflict to climax to resolution. The action usually begins at that moment in the story when the situation is already extreme and a climax in the making can already be felt. Most Greek tragedies observe the unities of time, place, and action. The time covered in an individual play is no more than one day, and the episodes happen in "real time," that is, if an episode takes ten minutes to perform, it is assumed to take ten minutes of fictional time as well. The odes, on the other hand, can be thought of as a kind of "time-out" in which real time is suspended. Unity of place means that only one setting is used per tragedy (an exception is Aeschylus' *Eumenides,* with two), and unity of action means one plot and one protagonist.

Our only surviving trilogy, the *Oresteia,* consists of the three tragedies *Agamemnon, The Libation Bearers,* and the *Eumenides.* Each of these plays has a unified linear plot, but the trilogy as a whole covers the events of several years. The three plays tell one story—the fate of the House of Atreus after the Trojan War. Since we have only one trilogy, it is impossible to generalize about the hundreds of others which were performed at the Festival of Dionysus. But we can observe that the endings of *Agamemnon* and *The Libation Bearers* do contain unresolved conflicts which seem to foreshadow further action, whereas in the *Eumenides* all conflict is resolved and an ideal world is restored. This fact may help us understand why many Greek tragedies are partially unresolved at the end; they are parts of trilogies with more plays to come.

In *Oedipus the King,* for instance, the question of Oedipus' future is left up in the air. He has decreed that Laius' murderer (Oedipus himself) must be exiled, and he continues to pursue this objective as the play ends, even though Creon, the new ruler, may be of another opinion. Furthermore, the obstacles to Oedipus' major objective of saving the city have been removed, but this potential resolution is not specifically dramatized. These unresolved issues strongly suggest that another play or two was meant to be performed after *Oedipus the King* at the festival in 430 B.C. When twenty-four years later Sophocles returned to this theme in *Oedipus at Colonus,* he ended the story on the same note of reconciliation we find at the end of the *Oresteia.* It would not be unreasonable to speculate that the 430 B.C. trilogy also had such an ending. In any case, the reader of *Oedipus the King* should be aware of the strong possibility that this play was performed as the beginning or middle section of a complete trilogy.

Because the Greek tragedians took all their characters from the same myths, many of the same names appear in a number of plays. But each author treats these familiar types in an individual way. The Creon of Sophocles' *Antigone* is a headstrong monarch who seeks to assert his authority in every sphere of human life, while the Creon of *Oedipus the King* is a well-balanced counselor who tries to persuade everyone to act reasonably. Euripides' Clytemnestra is a somewhat vain matron who pleads nervously for her life, while Aeschylus' Clytemnestra is an extremely powerful queen who stops at nothing, including murder, to make the world the way she wants it. It is best to approach each play freshly, without preconceptions, and learn what specific background and action the author has created for his particular version of the mythical character.

The protagonist in Greek tragedy often appears in every episode and does battle with a series of antagonists. In *Oedipus the King,* Oedipus finds himself in conflict with Teiresias, Creon, Jocasta, a messenger, and a shepherd. In *Antigone,* King Creon clashes with a guard, Antigone, his son Haimon, and Teiresias. Aeschylus, too, tends to follow this pattern which, in Euripides' plays, is subject to more variation. When the protagonist takes on one antagonist at a time we see his characteristic action—what he *does* about what he *wants*—from a number of perspectives and in a logical sequence which leads to the final facing of the truth.

The words *hubris* and *hamartia* are often used in connection with the characters of Greek tragedy. Hubris, sometimes defined as "arrogance," has more to do with what a character does than with what he is. While sailing to Troy to avenge the abduction of Helen, Agamemnon's fleet is becalmed in Aulis. Apollo will fill the sails with wind on one condition—that Agamemnon's daughter, Iphigenia, be offered as a blood sacrifice. In order to achieve his revengeful objective, Agamemnon commits this, and other, outrages, including the desecration of his enemy's sacred precincts. When he returns home to his wife he brings with him the Trojan princess Cassandra as his concubine and slave. Agamemnon's crowning hubristic act is to walk on a purple carpet which is spread along the path from his chariot to the palace steps. As he does so he seems dimly to realize his situation. "Let no god's eyes of hatred strike me from afar," he says as he sets foot on the exquisite fabric. But the gods see everything, especially the acts of hubristic mortals who seem to challenge their jealously guarded power. Within minutes, Agamemnon is murdered in the bath by his queen, Clytemnestra.

Although sometimes defined as "tragic flaw," *hamartia* is not so much a permanent feature of character as a tragic situation: the character is right in one way, but wrong in another. In the third episode of *Oedipus the King,* Oedipus accuses Creon of conspiring with Teiresias to pin the murder of Laius on him. Oedipus' character, at this point, could be formulated in this way: he is a king who accepts his responsibility and takes direct and unrelenting action to save his city. "Act as the crisis demands," he has declared, "and you shall have relief from all these evils." He now believes that the crisis demands the death of Creon on grounds of treason. But the audience knows better. We know that Oedipus is in the wrong, that Creon is innocent, and that Oedipus himself is guilty. But, given the urgency of the crisis and Oedipus' commitment to his objective, we can also empathize with his need to destroy the obstacles he finds in his way. Seeing that Oedipus is wrong, the Chorus of Theban Elders intervene in the conflict. When the *choragos* asks Oedipus to free Creon, he does so. Although sure he is right, Oedipus does not act on his belief, out of respect for the elders' viewpoint.

It is interesting to compare Oedipus' behavior with that of another King of Thebes in a similar situation. King Creon, in *Antigone,* also faces a grave civic crisis which requires swift action. Hoping to heal the war-torn city and restore order, Creon only succeeds in provoking greater disasters. Unlike Oedipus, Creon (in *Antigone*) treats the Theban Elders with contempt, calling them "doddering wrecks" and ignoring their advice until it is too late. Creon acts as if he has absolute, godlike power and knowledge and has no use for the wisdom or opinions of others—another example of hubris.

Resolution and Meaning

During the process of resolution, we begin to see the complete shape of the tragedy. In the final episode the protagonist, in suffering the consequences of his action, comes to recognize the power of Necessity. But he does not suffer in isolation. Through him the community—the other characters, the chorus, and

Elements of Greek Tragedy in the Television Commercial

Not only are the great majority of [television] commercials directly dramatic in nature (playlets of mere seconds' duration), but most of those that at first sight appear nondramatic contain the basic elements of fictional drama. Let us start with the most obviously dramatic kind of commercial, which usually follows a rigidly prescribed three-beat pattern. The sufferer from hemorrhoids, or bad breath, or an inability to make good coffee is near despair and appeals to a friend or relative for help; the friend draws the sufferer's attention to a product. There follows a moment of insight: this headache powder contains more of a painkilling ingredient than any other! this chewing gum fights bad breath more energetically! This moment of insight (the *anagnorisis* of classical drama) results in a reversal of fortune (the *peripeteia*) so that in the third beat we now find the erstwhile sufferer relieved, restored, and as a result blissfully happy, free from pain, anxiety, and guilt and able to make good coffee and thus capable of keeping her husband at home rather than have him roam the taverns in search of solace in drink or at the bosom of another woman, etc. This happy resolution is usually followed by the appearance of the product's symbol or trademark accompanied by a song or jingle, corresponding to the appearance in classical drama of the *deus ex machina* and the final choral ode that provide the resolution to apparently insoluble difficulties.

—Martin Esslin, *The Age of Television*

Martin Esslin uses Greek words to refer to several familiar elements of drama. Other Greek words for the elements of drama are *agon* (conflict), *mythos* (plot), *ethos* (character), *dianoia* (meaning), *pathos* (suffering or feeling), and *praxis* (action). The Greeks invented drama, and the concepts they used still work today, although sometimes with a different emphasis.

the audience in the theatre—suffer also and share a public vision of universal reality. Greek tragedy offered its audience nothing less than a lifting of the veil of appearances and an opportunity to face and survive the truth of human existence.

As contemporary readers of Greek tragedy, we may feel that we face different truths than did the Greek audiences twenty-five hundred years ago. How, then, do we create meaning from these plays? How do we reconcile the tensions which exist between the fictional images of life the Greeks presented and the ongoing reality of our own lives? One way to begin is to identify particular areas in which the view of life implied in Greek tragedy differs from our own. The discovery that it is possible to look at life through entirely new eyes is in itself a kind of meaning which drama has to offer.

We live in an age in which the idea of truth is linked to the process of scientific investigation. Truth is available for us, not now, but at some time in the future, when all the experiments have been performed and all the data are in. The implication of Greek tragedy, however, is that a form of truth is immediately available to those who are willing to face it and strong enough to survive. Since most mortals prefer their daily illusions, this willingness and strength must come from the tragic protagonist. Characters such as Oedipus, Creon, Electra, and Orestes undertake extreme, audacious objectives and pursue them relentlessly, to the point of catastrophe. Their actions help the community to face its fear of the implacable power of Necessity and inspire pity for the suffering which they must undergo in the process. If we empathize with the tragic protagonist, we can vicariously test our own powers of truth facing and survival.

Another difference between the world of Greek tragedy and our own is the issue of fair play. Most of us, like Miss Prism in *The Importance of Being Earnest,* like to see the good end happily and the bad unhappily. But life, in Greek tragedy, is not fair. When Athena casts the deciding vote in Orestes' trial in the *Eumenides* she says, in effect, that killing a husband is worse than killing a mother; thus, the principles of patriarchy are affirmed in Athens. In Euripides' *Medea,* the jealous protagonist murders her children and flies away in a chariot at the end. And, in that author's *Bacchae,* Pentheus and Agave are destroyed because they do not recognize Dionysus, although he is in disguise and does nothing to reveal himself. Necessity is often cruel and indifferent to mortal notions of justice. Miss Prism would probably not approve of most Greek tragedy.

In *Oedipus at Colonus,* Oedipus, now an old man, reflects on the injustice he has endured at the hands of the gods:

Tell me this: if there were prophecies
Repeated by the oracles of the gods,
That father's death should come through his own son,
How could you justly blame it on me?
On me, who was yet unborn, yet unconceived,
Not yet existent for my father and mother?

Oedipus took every action he could, throughout his life, to avoid evil and to serve Thebes. And yet, at the height of his powers, he had to face the catastrophic reality of his true condition, and then endure blindness and exile to the end of his days. In this play (Sophocles' last, written at the age of ninety), Oedipus' suffering and his long life come to an end in the same mysterious moment:

> MESSENGER: But in what manner
> Oedipus perished, no one of mortal men
> Could tell but Theseus. It was not lightning,
> Bearing its fire from God, that took him off;
> No hurricane was blowing.
> But some attendant from the train of Heaven
> Came for him; or else the underworld
> Opened in love the unlit door of earth.
> For he was taken without lamentation,
> Illness or suffering; indeed his end
> Was wonderful if ever mortal's was.

Subject all his life to the terrible power of Necessity, perhaps Oedipus, at the end, becomes a part of that force which is beyond good and evil, happiness or unhappiness.

Whether or not we actually accept the seemingly harsh idea of Necessity, it helps to read Greek tragedy as if we do. In this way, we may be able to look at the realities of life on Earth in the late twentieth century from a Greek perspective. Does our life simply move back and forth between the poles of happiness and unhappiness, justice and injustice, good and evil? Or would Aeschylus, Sophocles, or Euripides, brought back to life in our time, be able to show us a more fundamental principle which reconciles these apparent opposites?

A Checklist

READING GREEK TRAGEDY

- *What is the situation?*
  Greek tragedy usually begins with an extreme situation. Something is deeply wrong or some kind of disturbing news has just been received. It is important to identify this element as soon as possible. Greek tragedy is highly condensed, and all character and choric behavior is related to one central situation.

- *Who are the protagonist(s) and antagonist(s)?*
  Who is doing something about the situation? Who is opposing this character or characters?

- *What is the main conflict in each episode?*
  How is this conflict built up from smaller conflicts? What larger underlying conflict do the episodes reveal?

- *Who are the chorus and how do they respond to the situation?*
  Choral response is of two kinds. They interact with the characters in the episodes and act as a model audience in the odes. Kinds of Greek choral behavior are prayer, lament, joyous celebration, contemplation, and sharing of ironic insight or wisdom. Remember that the chorus are always a part of dramatic space after the *parodos*. Audience anticipation of their response to the action can be imagined as part of the theatre event.

- *What truths are faced in the course of the action?*
  What hidden identities, objectives, or obstacles are revealed? The recognition of these things usually leads to some kind of suffering in the final episode. Does this suffering imply or lead to recognition, for characters or audience, of the operation of supernatural or universal forces?

11 ❧ Shakespeare

Shakespeare worked without knowing he would become Shakespeare.

—Colette, French novelist

*T*he first thing we usually hear about Shakespeare is his reputation. He may very well be the greatest cultural celebrity in world history. Whole industries in entertainment, bookselling, tourism, and literary criticism and scholarship have been, and continue to be, based on his dramas. But contemplating Shakespeare's fame, well deserved as it is, may not be the best way to learn how to read his plays. In fact, his fame may even get in the way. Majestic cultural monuments can be intimidating and, if we fail to make the right human connection, end by disappointing us. Another approach to Shakespearean drama is to take a look at how his professional circumstances shaped his scripts.

During the twenty years or so of his working life, William Shakespeare was involved in three separate aspects of the theatre. For one, he was a "sharer" in a company of actors called the Lord Chamberlain's Men. This meant that he was one of an inner circle of six or eight actors who determined the company's artistic and business policies and shared the profits. He was also part owner of the Globe Theatre and shared those consequent responsibilities and revenues as well. In addition, he was the company poet. This meant that he supplied his fellow actors with the popular comedies, tragedies, histories, and romances which were the cornerstone of their success and led them, finally, to gain the patronage of King James I, who changed their name to the King's Men. Shakespeare's three-way participation in the professional theatre enabled the hardworking actor-playwright-businessman to buy a house in London and a handsome piece of property in his native Stratford, where he began his retirement at the age of forty-eight.

Shakespeare's professional life, then, was lived in the world of practical theatre. He was not a writer of books. Although he was concerned with how his poetry appeared in print, he apparently took little interest in the publication of his plays, which were, in any case, no longer his once they were sold to an acting company. In fact, of the three dozen or so dramas that came from his pen, only half were published in his lifetime. It was not until 1623, seven years after Shakespeare's death, that two of his fellow actors, John Heminge and Henry Condell, published his complete dramatic works. In the First Folio, as this volume is called, many of Shakespeare's greatest plays appeared in print for the first time. Since the publication of the First Folio, a long tradition of highly specialized scholarship has grown up around the publication of the plays and is being given new life in the computer age. The Shakespearean scripts we read today have been analyzed and edited with great skill and painstaking attention. But they are based on a body of work which was, for Shakespeare, not the stuff of books, but a way of filling the Globe Theatre with dramatic action.

We will probably never be able to say exactly how every scene of Shakespeare's plays was originally staged. But a general understanding of the Globe Theatre can get us into the spirit of the kind of theatrical event Shakespeare was trying to create. By keeping the stage in mind as we read, we can interpret dialogue and stage directions, connect with the characters, and imagine dramatic space and the audience's role from a more Shakespearean point of view.

Shakespeare's Globe

As we have seen from the excerpt from *Hamlet* in Script 8, all the Shakespearean theatre event needs is an actor and some space. But, although Shakespeare's company did sometimes play in improvised surroundings, their home theatre was an elaborate structure. The heart of the Globe Theatre was a large platform stage from which Shakespeare and his company inspired the communal imagination of their audience mainly through the power of the spoken word. Behind this stage was a four-story structure with a twofold function. It served the players as a *tiring house,* that is, a backstage area for dressing and awaiting cues, as well as for the production of music and sound effects; and, from the public's point of view, it served as a permanent basic setting for all the plays. This structure was joined on either side by the gallery, a three-tiered ring of boxes which rose vertically on three sides of the stage. Some privileged spectators entered by the stage door, mingled with the actors backstage and, during the performance, occupied boxes in the tiring house or sat on the stage. But most of the audience entered through the main door and either stood in the brick-paved pit or, for an extra charge, took seats in the gallery. Exposed to winter and summer weather, those in the pit, called "groundlings," paid a penny to stand while enjoying the "three-hours traffic" of the play. The Globe Theatre was a unified space in which spectators and actors were visible to one another in natural light.

Momentum and Setting

Shakespeare's action moves from scene to scene without interruption. The act and scene divisions found in his scripts are for the convenience of the reader and do not indicate any physical change in the performance space. The end of one scene is followed immediately by the beginning of another. There were no pauses for scene changes or even intermissions at the Globe. It is very important to keep this principle of momentum in mind while reading. One way to do this is to imagine that characters who are leaving begin to move offstage while they are still talking and that entering characters start to talk before they are completely onstage.

Shakespeare's scripts also offer a great range of setting. The many levels and openings of the tiring house in combination with the large stage gave Shakespeare everything he needed to move the action instantaneously from place to place. Characters could appear from or disappear into the various openings in the tiring house or even fly in from the heavens and vanish under the stage. Designed by actors who had mastered their craft and who knew the importance of actor-audience interplay, the Globe was one of the most versatile theatres ever built.

This versatility meant that Shakespeare could write plays with many settings and no scenery. The Globe could produce *Antony and Cleopatra,* with its forty scenes set "in several parts of the Roman Empire," as easily as *The Comedy of Errors,* with eleven scenes set in the town of Ephesus. Except for movable items such as banners, thrones, weapons, beds, and the like, the theatre would look basically the same for both plays. The Globe audience simply imagined whatever places were necessary to the action. "Let us," says the Prologue of *Henry V* to this audience, "on your imaginary forces work." Settings such as "a room in the castle," "a churchyard," or "Bosworth field" are important indicators of occasion and situation but have little significance in terms of physical environment. The stage itself is the environment for the continuous action of Shakespearean drama.

The excerpts from *Hamlet* in Script 10 show how Shakespeare may have used various parts of the Globe Theatre as setting. The general locale of the play is Elsinore Castle in Denmark. The most frequent settings are "the castle platform," "another part of the platform," "a room in the castle," and "another room in the castle." Since the players had a three-story scenic facade as well as twelve hundred square feet of stage to work with, this kind of variety was not a problem. The stage, moreover, was equipped with two large pillars, which helped to divide the space when division was needed.

In excerpt A, the actor playing the Ghost (believed by some to be Shakespeare himself) is actually under the stage—"in the cellarage," as Hamlet says. In B, the "traps"—removable pieces of platform that gave access to the cellarage—are used to indicate a grave. Symbolizing the earth, the grave, purgatory, and hell, the traps were complemented by the "heavens," a mural of sun, stars, clouds, and signs of the zodiac painted on the underside of the stage roof (the shadow), which sheltered the actors from the real sun, rain, and snow. The actor playing Hamlet (C) is able to refer ("look you") to both the painted heavens and the real sky, which is partly visible to all. Used several times in the play, the "arras" (D) could very well be a tapestry covering a stage-level opening in the tiring house—the "inner below." The "noise within" and the Messenger could also come from this opening, as if it were a door to the king's room. When Fortinbras and his force arrive at the end of the play (E), they could enter from the inner above and other openings above stage

Script 10
Setting in Shakespeare's
Hamlet

A. Under the Stage

GHOST [*cries under the stage*]: Swear.
HAMLET: Ha, ha, boy! art thou there, truepenny? Come on,—you hear
this fellow in the cellarage,—Consent to swear.

B. The Traps

[LAERTES *leaps in the grave. . . .* HAMLET *leaps in after* LAERTES. *. . . The*
Attendants *part them, and they come out of the grave.*]

C. The Stage Roof

HAMLET: . . . and indeed it goes so heavily with my disposition that this
goodly frame, the earth, seems to me a sterile promontory; this
most excellent canopy, the air, look you, this brave o'erhanging
firmament, this majestical roof fretted with golden fire . . .

D. The Inner Below

QUEEN: Withdraw, I hear him coming.
[POLONIUS *hides behind the arras.*]

[*A noise within.*]
QUEEN: Alack, what noise is this?
[*Enter a* Messenger]
KING: Where are my Switzers? Let them guard the door.

E. The Inner Above

[*Enter* FORTINBRAS *and* ENGLISH AMBASSADOR, *with drum, colors and*
Attendants.]

level, as the stage itself is by now full of courtiers and corpses. Since Fortinbras
is the new King of Denmark, this place of prominence would be appropriate. It
would also be a good place from which to oversee the final procession:

FORTINBRAS: Take up the bodies. Such a sight as this becomes the field,
but here shows much amiss. Go bid the soldiers shoot.
[*Exeunt marching, after which a peal of ordnance is shot off.*]

Here the dramatic space probably includes the entire stage and tiring house.
The Globe Theatre was well suited to such panoramic scenes. Pro-
cessionals, ceremonies, and battles abound in Shakespeare's scripts. Skilled

in combat as well as in music and dancing, and sparing no expense in the costume and props department, his players were well prepared to fill the stage with a full spectrum of physical activity.

The Play and the Audience

Unlike the Greek theatre event, in which the chorus occupied a middle ground between actor and audience, the actors themselves made direct contact with the audience at the Globe Theatre. An actor standing in the middle of the platform stage could command instant attention from the two thousand spectators in the wraparound auditorium. He could engage in earthy exchanges with the groundlings in the pit, share subtle thoughts and feelings with the patrons in the vertically tiered galleries, or harangue the whole theatre and whatever spirits of nature or cosmic forces might also be hovering in the sky above the open roof of the playhouse. Shakespeare's scripts are full of moments of actor-audience contact. But the kind of mediating between audience and play we saw in the Greek choral odes is now frequently integrated into the action.

In Shakespeare, actor-audience contacts fall into three categories. First, there are the formally designated choruses and prologues which give us background and guidelines to response. These choric characters seem to stand outside the dramatic action, contemplating the play and describing it to the audience. A second category includes asides and soliloquies. In these, the character speaks from within the action. Although still caught up in the pursuit of an objective, the character takes a momentary time-out to share thoughts and feelings with the audience. In a third, more complicated, instance the character is involved in the dramatic action and in choric behavior at the same time.

Choruses and Prologues

Choruses and prologues introduce the audience to the play, provide information from time to time, and summarize the action at the play's conclusion. Shakespeare and his fellow Elizabethans got their idea of the chorus from their favorite Roman tragedian, Seneca, who in turn adopted it from the Greeks. But in Shakespeare, as in Seneca, the chorus is a single actor, not a group of performers. Nor does a chorus, or prologue, appear at predictable intervals in every play, as in Greek tragedy. In Shakespeare's freewheeling dramatic style, derived as much from medieval as from Greek and Roman models, choric behavior can appear anywhere, at any time. *Romeo and Juliet* has a chorus at the beginning and in the middle, but the final speech is assigned to the Prince, who sounds so much like the chorus that the two parts are often played by the same actor. In *Henry V,* the chorus introduces the play as "Prologue," then appears as "Chorus" at the middle and end. This well-known prologue, besides supplying necessary background, asks for collaboration between actor and audience. "Let us," he says, "on your imaginary forces work." And he goes on to teach us how to get the most out of a performance of *Henry V* at the Globe:

> **Suppose** within the girdle of these walls
> Are now confined two mighty monarchies
> Whose high upreared and abutting fronts
> The perilous narrow ocean parts asunder.
> Piece out our imperfections **with your thoughts:**
> Into a thousand parts divide one man
> And make **imaginary** puissance [power].
> **Think,** when we talk of horses, **that you see them**
> Printing their proud hoofs i' th' receiving earth:
> **For 'tis your thoughts** that now must deck our kings . . .

To suppose, to think, to imagine—this is the role, not only of the audience at *Henry V,* but of the reader of any of Shakespeare's plays. Halfway through *Henry V* this same actor, now promoted to chorus, helps us with a change of setting:

> The King is set from London, and the scene
> Is now transported, gentles, to Southampton.
> There is the playhouse now, there must you sit.

And he also shows up at the end to deliver an epilogue, reminding the audience of the patriotic significance of the play.

Asides and Soliloquies

Asides and soliloquies are spoken by characters fully engaged in the dramatic action. As we saw in Part One, the aside is spoken in the presence of other characters, but unheard by them. Hamlet's first line is an aside:

HAMLET [*aside*]:   A little more than kin and less than kind.

In the dramatic space with Hamlet are most of the characters of the play, assembled before the throne of the newly crowned and wed King and Queen of Denmark. By ignoring this splendid company and speaking first to us, Hamlet immediately establishes a special relationship with the audience, which is developed throughout the play in that most interesting and subtle form of direct address, the soliloquy.

With a few rare exceptions, only one character is present in the dramatic space during a soliloquy. Time stops and the character invites the audience into his company. The ways in which this can happen are several and are open to reader and actor interpretation. The character may talk to himself and allow us to overhear. He may address the universe and include us as part of it. He may confide in a single audience member and leave the rest of us to eavesdrop. He can treat us coldly, warmly, contemptuously, ingratiatingly—the behavioral possibilities in soliloquies are as varied as in any other kind of dramatic action. In reading soliloquies, we should remember that the character is not reading a speech. Imagination and empathic connection are as important here as elsewhere. The crucial factor in soliloquies, however they are interpreted, is interplay with the audience. It is almost as if the character, for a change, is trying to make empathic connection with us.

Choric and Character Behavior

A dramatic character may also interact with other characters in the dramatic space and, at the same time, comment on the action as if he were on the outside looking in. The Prince in *Romeo and Juliet* does this. His six lines end the play:

A glooming peace this morning with it brings.	1
The Sun, for sorrow, will not show his head.	2
Go hence, to have more talk of these sad things;	3
Some shall be pardoned, and some punished;	4
For never was a story of more woe	5
Than this of Juliet and her Romeo.	6

The role of Prince here combines character and choric behavior. In lines 1 and 2 he describes the setting, as a prologue might. In lines 3 and 4 he behaves like a ruler giving orders. In lines 5 and 6 he sums things up, in the manner of a chorus.

Another example of a character whose behavior has choric aspects is found in *Hamlet,* when Rosencrantz reflects on the downfall of kings. Sharing the dramatic space with Guildenstern and King Claudius himself, Rosencrantz seems to speak to them and to the audience at the same time:

> The cease [decease] of majesty
> Dies not alone, but like a gulf [whirlpool] doth draw
> What's near it with it. It is a massy [massive] wheel
> Fix'd on the summit of the highest mount,
> To whose huge spokes ten thousand lesser things
> Are mortis'd and adjoin'd; which when it falls,
> Each small annexment, petty consequence,
> Attends the boist'rous ruin. Never alone
> Did the king sigh, but with a general groan.

These sentences have little to do with the immediate objective or with Rosencrantz's typical behavior. The king, who speaks next, does not even acknowledge the speech. But it does articulate for the audience a general response to the spectacle of royal disarray as well as a portent of impending disaster.

Such passages, which function simultaneously as action and chorus, are frequently found in the Shakespearean script, and if we bear in mind the continuing interaction between play and audience, their function will be clearer. What's more, this kind of behavior still exists in contemporary life. Think of the master of ceremonies who praises the commencement speaker to his face but is really talking to the assembled audience. He is combining two kinds of behavior: he is greeting and praising the guest of honor; and he is also, like a chorus, telling the audience who this guest is and how we should respond to him. (Rosencrantz's generalizations about the fall of kings is much less flattering to Claudius than the typical introduction of a guest of honor.) Shakespearean theatre was a public event, more like a session of Congress or a courtroom trial than a movie or even a contemporary, live dramatic performance.

Shakespeare's Dialogue

In learning to read Shakespeare, a good first rule is *have patience*. The English language has undergone many changes since these plays were first performed, and even scholars who have devoted their lives to studying them do not understand everything. Second, learn to use notes and glossaries when you really *need* to know something—which may be quite often—but avoid getting bogged down in word-by-word analysis of the script. Momentum is very important in Shakespeare, and you should try to stay up to speed, even if you have to skip difficult passages the first time through. Analytical time is better spent deciphering the human, rather than the linguistic, aspects of the dialogue. And, finally, follow the same procedure you would use in reading any script. Find out who's there, where they are, what they're doing, and what's new or wrong. Discover the characters' objectives, what stands in their way, and what they do about it. Above all, connect with the human behavior and let your understanding grow from there.

Shakespearean dialogue, like all classical dialogue, performs a multitude of functions. It gives full and coherent expression to the characters' thoughts and feelings, contains streams of imagery that evoke setting and atmosphere, provides details of occasion and situation, and constructs a moral or philosophical framework in which the action can be viewed.

First of all, however, Shakespearean dialogue often provides simple, direct expression of physical activity in the form of what we might call *gestural* dialogue. The following lines from various plays of Shakespeare provide the reader with an immediate sense of human presence:

HORATIO: Well, sit we down, and let us hear Bernardo speak of this.

ROMEO: Give me that mattock and the wrenching iron.

Script 11
From Shakespeare's
A Midsummer Night's Dream

Who's there? Oberon, King of the Fairies, and his servant, Puck.
Setting. A wood near Athens.
Occasion. Oberon is giving Puck careful orders.
Situation. Oberon, with help from Puck, wants to punish his Queen, Titania, for disobedience. And Puck sometimes gets things wrong.

[*Exeunt* TITANIA *and her followers.*]
OBERON: **Well, go thy way:** thou shalt not from this grove
　　Till I torment thee for this injury.
　　My gentle Puck, come hither. Thou rememb'rest
　　Since once I sat upon a promontory
　　And heard a mermaid, on a dolphin's back,　　　　　5
　　Uttering such dulcet and harmonious breath
　　That the rude sea grew civil at her song
　　And certain stars shot madly from their spheres
　　To hear the sea-maid's music?
PUCK: **I remember.**　　　　　　　　　　　　　　　10
OBERON: **That very time I saw** (but thou couldst not)
　　Flying between the cold moon and the earth,
　　Cupid, all armed. A certain aim he took
　　At a fair Vestal, throned by the West.
　　And loosed his love-shaft smartly from his bow,　　15
　　As it should pierce a hundred thousand hearts.
　　But I might see [then I saw] young Cupid's fiery shaft
　　Quenched in the chaste beams of the watery moon,
　　And the imperial vot'ress passed on,
　　In maiden meditation, fancy-free.　　　　　　　　20
　　Yet marked I where the bolt of Cupid fell.
　　It fell upon a little Western flower,
　　Before milk-white, now purple with love's wound,
　　And maidens call it love-in-idleness.
　　Fetch me that flow'r . . .　　　　　　　　　　25

Paraphrase of *A Midsummer Night's Dream*

LINE NO.	CHARACTER OBJECTIVE	PARAPHRASE OF DIALOGUE
1–2	Oberon wants to punish Titania.	All right, leave if you like. But I'll get back at you before you leave the wood.
3	Oberon wants to give Puck an important assignment.	Come here, Puck.
3–9	Oberon wants to focus his thoughts and clarify them to Puck.	Do you remember the time we heard a mermaid singing? Do you remember how her song calmed the sea and how the stars fell from the sky as she sang?
10	Puck wants to cooperate with and encourage Oberon.	
11–20	Oberon wants to dramatize the memory and gradually reveal his reasons for bringing it up now.	Well, I saw something else you couldn't see. I saw Cupid with his bow flying through the sky. He aimed his arrow at a young virgin and shot it toward her with great force; but the arrow missed and the girl went away as innocently as before.
21	Now Oberon wants to fix Puck's attention on the purpose of the talk.	I carefully watched Cupid's arrow and noted where it fell.
22–24	Oberon wants to be certain that the details are absolutely clear to Puck, because he is coming to the point of his story.	The arrow hit a flower and changed its color from white (innocence) to purple (sexual desire). The flower is nick-named "love-in-idleness" (having sexual potential) by virgin girls.
25	Having got Puck's complete attention, Oberon comes to the point.	

KING: Let him go, Gertrude. Speak, man.

QUINCE: Is all our company here?

LEAR: Pray you, undo this button.

Short, rhythmic sequences also embody vivid physical conflict, as in this fencing passage from *Hamlet* in which we hear, in our mind's ear, the clash of the foils:

HAMLET: Come on, sir.

LAERTES: Come, my lord.

[*They fence.*]

HAMLET: One.

LAERTES: No.

HAMLET: Judgment.

OSRIC: A hit, a very palpable hit.

This gestural dialogue helps us keep our bearings in the script. It gives strong, simple answers to questions of occasion and situation. If we know what the characters are doing physically, we can see where the more subtle behavior in the scene is coming from.

For example, finding the lines of gestural dialogue is the key to Script 11. These simple lines provide an outline of the action:

Well, go thy way.

My gentle Puck, come hither.

Thou rememb'rest.

I remember.

Fetch me that flow'r.

Oberon bids Titania an angry farewell, conspires with a willing Puck, and plots to acquire a magic flower with which he can humiliate Titania. (The flower will cause her to desire the first creature she sees when she wakes up.) Having established this outline, we can delve deeper into the scene by (1) analyzing the small objectives by which Oberon pursues his larger goal and (2) paraphrasing the dialogue in terms of these objectives (see Script 11). In a paraphrase we put the dialogue in our own words. Although paraphrase is bound to distort the original, it is a useful intermediate step.

Even though Oberon is a supernatural character, we can still empathize (although not everyone may sympathize) with his intense desire to punish the woman who has made him angry and jealous. We can also follow the steps he takes to enlist Puck in his project. Since Puck is not always reliable, Oberon takes pains to explain exactly what he wants and to be sure Puck understands what he's talking about. (Readers who know the play will recognize a subtle conflict in this scene between the egotistical demands of Oberon and the free-spirited attitude of Puck.) Oberon also takes a sensual pleasure in plotting revenge. This sensuality is expressed through the music of the language and cannot be paraphrased. Shakespeare's musicality should be viewed as an aspect of dramatic behavior, and not just as decoration.

Once we have established the action in the script, it is much easier to appreciate the rhythms and sounds of Shakespeare's dialogue. Shakespearean language operates in a sensual and physical way. It was written to be spoken, and speech is a physical as well as an intellectual activity. Through his actors, Shakespeare had to compel the attention of thousands of patrons, and to do so he used two strategies. First, he created patterns of tension and release by alternating verse and prose. The formality and intensity of verse seized the audience's attention, while the informality of colloquial prose relaxed them. Second, the verse itself echoes the familiar rhythms of pulse and breathing and verges, sometimes, on the more overt rhythms of chanting, singing, or other kinds of repetitive vocal exertion. If we tune in on the beat of Shakespeare's dialogue we will connect physically with his drama.

What kind of verse did Shakespeare write for his actors? In the days before the Globe was built, actors on outdoor stages, with lungs like bellows, thundered out a line called the *fourteener:*

> O father dear, these words to hear—that you must die by
>   force—
> Bedews my cheeks with stilled tears. The king hath no remorse.

The fourteener was so called because each line had fourteen syllables. When the actors moved indoors, a swifter, handier line replaced the bludgeonlike beat of the fourteener. It was called the iambic pentameter. It had only ten syllables per line—the actors could breathe more often—and each line was divided into five (pentameter) two-syllable units called *feet*. The typical foot was an iamb—an unstressed syllable followed by a stressed syllable. The great pioneer of iambic pentameter was Christopher Marlowe:

> Was **this** the **face** that **launched** a **thou**sand **ships**
> And **burnt** the **top**less **towers** of **I**lium

If we read these lines aloud without overstressing, we can feel the beat in the background of the idea.

Shakespeare's iambic pentameter is an extremely supple line and should be read with primary attention to the meaning. But the background beat will often clarify the sense, and it is especially helpful in reminding readers to stress the last syllable of the line, where the main idea usually is made complete. Unlike Marlowe, Shakespeare does not always end his thought and his line at the same time, although stressing the last word helps hold the thought as we turn the corner into the next line:

> Tis now the very witching time of **night**,
> When churchyards yawn, and hell itself breathes **out**

We have to go to the third line in this speech to make sense of the second:

> When churchyards yawn, and hell itself breathes **out**
> Contagion to this world. Now could I drink hot **blood**

This "run-on" line requires the reader both to maintain the stress on "out" and to follow the sense into the next line, which has an extra foot in it ("hot blood"). But never mind; Shakespeare will usually put feeling before form, a habit which his neoclassical critics condemned but which readers and actors appreciate. The passage continues:

> Now could I drink hot **blood**
> And do such bitter business as the **day**

Another run-on line; but the stress on "day" echoes that on "night" in the first line, giving symmetry to the speech.

> And do such bitter business as the **day**
> Would quake to look on. Soft! Now to my **mother!**

"Soft! Now to my mother!" is very gestural in feeling. It releases the tension of thought through the impulse to physical activity and seems to break free of the iambic pentameter line entirely. The final stress on "mother" focuses Hamlet's, and the reader's, attention on the climactic scene to come.

Another crucial facet of Shakespeare's dialogue is wordplay. Because Shakespeare's audience did not read, but listened to, his plays, words existed primarily as sounds. And Shakespeare uses the sounds of English to stimulate the ear with lightninglike wordplay in which single sounds illuminate multiple images in the mind. In Script 8, when Hamlet asks the First Player, "Com'st thou to beard me in Denmark?" the word *beard* brings these images to mind: the Player's actual beard, the idea that Hamlet himself might be looking for a disguise, and the inference that the Player might be offering him some personal challenge. (All of these things, in fact, come true in the course of the play.) When Francisco, in the opening moment of *Hamlet,* demands that Bernardo "unfold" himself, he announces a major aspect of the play's action: the souls of the characters are hidden and must be revealed. The Ghost echoes this word when he threatens to "unfold" the mysteries of the soul's afterlife. When Laertes threatens him, the king claims he is protected by a "hedge" of divinity. The audience, knowing of his evil deeds, may also foresee that he will soon be "hedged" in another sense, that is, thwarted by divine will. The "judgment" Hamlet calls for in his duel with Laertes echoes his sustained inner need to see the rottenness of the Danish state healed by divine judgment. Far from being just a playful trick, Shakespearean wordplay alerts the mind to multiple levels of meaning in the dramatic action.

Conflict and Recognition

Unlike Greek tragedy, in which the action is simple and direct, Shakespearean drama is intricate and multidirectional. In Greek tragedy, the protagonist takes direct action to overcome the obstacles to his objective. The action of a Shakespearean tragedy, in contrast, is generated by the interaction of two characters who are in conflict with one another but who nevertheless pursue a common objective. The function of protagonist is divided between these two characters; one is the instigator of the conflict and the other is the agent. The instigator has a clear and dynamic vision of the objective but does not act directly to remove the obstacle. Instead, the instigator persuades, entices, flatters, exhorts, bullies, or deceives another character, the agent, into taking action. This agent-protagonist both resists the instigator and acts to overcome the obstacles, which means that the agent is also in conflict with himself. This complex structuring creates conflict at three levels: the instigator **wants** the agent to act in pursuit of a common objective, **but** the agent resists. Instigator and agent both **want** to achieve a common objective, **but** other characters resist them. The agent **wants** to achieve the objective, **but** he also has doubts about the validity of the objective.

Rather than look for a single protagonist, then, we should seek the source of Shakespeare's tragic conflict in the instigator-agent relationship. For instance, Lady Macbeth wants Macbeth to become King of Scotland. Macbeth both resists her and carries out her objective by murdering Duncan, the present king. Three conflicts, then, ignite the action of Macbeth: Lady Macbeth vs. Macbeth; Macbeth and Lady Macbeth vs. the Scottish nobility; Macbeth vs. himself. *Othello* provides another example of this pattern. Iago wants to destroy Othello by convincing him that his wife, Desdemona, is unfaithful. Othello resists Iago's moves but finally becomes the agent of his own self-destruction by murdering the innocent Desdemona. The three conflicts of *Othello* are Iago vs. Othello, Iago and Othello vs. Desdemona, and Othello vs. himself. In *Hamlet,* the Ghost wants to take revenge against his murderer, King Claudius. Hamlet both resists the Ghost's purpose and achieves his objective, producing three conflicts: Hamlet vs. the Ghost; Hamlet and the Ghost vs. Claudius; Hamlet vs. himself. The pivotal character in this structure is the agent-protagonist, who is involved in all three aspects of the conflict. Other examples of characters who function in this way are Brutus in *Julius Caesar,* Antony in *Antony and Cleopatra,* and King Lear, who becomes the agent of his own self-destruction, instigated by his daughters Goneril and Reagan. In *Romeo and Juliet,* Romeo becomes the unwitting agent of two feuding families, bringing about a death on each side and his own banishment.

What kind of recognition does this three-faceted conflict produce? Although Shakespearean drama contains moments of many kinds of recognition, there is usually one key moment, somewhere in the middle of the play, when the agent-protagonist sees, or believes he sees, the true nature of his situation. Macbeth faces a sustained and harrowing vision of his predicament when he sees, first, the ghost of his enemy Banquo and, then, a parade of apparitions which show him the future kings of Scotland, all Banquo's descendants. Othello wrongly believes he has discovered a false wife in Desdemona and a true ally in Iago. "Now art thou my lieutenant," he tells Iago, after they have knelt together and sworn mutual loyalty. "O I am fortune's fool," says Romeo when he realizes that he is partly responsible for the murder of his kinsman, Mercutio, and has just killed Juliet's kinsman, Tybalt. Hamlet recognizes both his problem and its solution while watching the First Player perform. He shares this discovery with us in soliloquy:

> The play's the thing
> Wherein I'll catch the conscience of the king.

This approach to conflict and recognition is also found in the comedies, in which lovers use agents to pursue the objects of their affections or disguise themselves and become the agents of others' love plots, and so produce the tangle of mistaken objectives and obstacles that is a hallmark of Shakespearean comedy. Moments of recognition include the throwing off of disguises, revealing the true identity of one or more lovers, and removing the final obstacle to the triumph of young love.

Plot and Character

Plot, in general, is a pattern of action. In Shakespeare, the word takes on an additional shade of meaning—conspiracy. Because conflict springs from the interaction of instigator and agent and because agent-protagonists frequently employ subagents to pursue their objectives, most Shakespearean plots are networks of conspiracy, and most major Shakespearean characters are plotters of one kind or another. In *Hamlet*, for instance, the Ghost, Hamlet, King Claudius, and Polonius all instigate plots against one another with separate, but convergent, objectives. Hamlet is also the agent of the Ghost and Polonius, that of the King. In addition, Rosencrantz and Guildenstern become agents of Polonius, and the Players act as agents of Hamlet. In the final scene, Laertes is the agent of the King and only Hamlet is acting, at last, on his own behalf. The careful reader will be sure to keep track of who's on whose side and who's pretending to be on one side but is actually on another. This information is often revealed in a brief moment at the beginning or end of a scene, when one character takes another to one side (behind one of the stage pillars, perhaps) and contrives or reveals a conspiracy.

Another important feature of the Shakespearean plot is the midplay climax, usually coinciding with a moment of recognition. In most of the non-Shakespearean examples of drama we have investigated so far, the climax comes near the end of the play, followed by a comparatively brief dénouement. In Shakespearean tragedy, a major climax, which reverses the situation, usually occurs near the middle of the play. This climax is followed by a long dénouement, sometimes called the "falling action." Since tragedy was meant to represent, in part, the fall of the mighty, we may assume that Shakespeare's audience liked to watch them fall a long way. The falling action usually includes further climaxes and a widening recognition of universal truths, somewhat resembling the perception of Necessity through suffering in the last episode of Greek tragedy.

Shakespearean drama, however, is rooted in a Christian, not a Greek, view of the human situation, which means that a struggle between good and evil is usually part of the action. A number of important Shakespearean characters are clearly associated with the forces of evil, especially Richard III and Iago. Macbeth and Claudius also ally themselves with the powers of darkness, although neither really enjoys this alliance as much as do Richard and Iago. Joan of Arc, usually depicted in drama as a saint, is presented as an evil witch by Shakespeare in *Henry VI, Part I*, a play of anti-French sentiment and English patriotism.

One of the great heroes of Shakespearean drama is Prince Hal, who becomes Henry V, saviour of England. Hamlet, too, has heroic aspects. He strives to act within a carefully considered ethical framework, he is respectful of the forces of salvation and damnation, and he prudently considers the possibility that the apparition of the Ghost may be a trick of the devil to draw him into sin. The youthful and innocent lovers, Romeo and Juliet, teach their elders to amend their murderous ways through the purity of their love. Indeed, Shakespeare's lovers in general, but especially the women, are of an heroic cast, although they may sometimes be temporarily lacking in good sense. Good men gone wrong are also present in such characters as Othello, Macbeth, and Antony.

But Shakespeare's characters are usually larger and more complicated than the framework of good and evil in which they are presented. Macbeth and Claudius, as mentioned, are at war with the evil in themselves. Falstaff (*Henry IV, Part One*), whose sinful ways tarnish the princely reputation of his friend Hal, manages to be one of Shakespeare's most sympathetic characters; Shakespeare also gives us reason to sympathize with the mean-spirited and scheming Shylock (*The Merchant of Venice*). Even Iago and Richard III have their redeeming qualities—both are brilliant, articulate, and entertaining. As Hamlet reminds us, "The devil hath power to assume a pleasing shape." Although the struggle between good and evil is always present in Shakespeare, the characters on both sides are presented without prejudice, in the fullness of their humanity.

If Shakespeare is not judgmental in his view of human character, neither is he sentimental. After Hamlet kills Polonius, he tells the corpse, in short, that it got what it deserved, and then he turns immediately to a conversation with his mother. Malvolio, in *Twelfth Night*, is punished painfully and at length for his pretentious and overbearing attitude. The innocence of the heroines of *Hamlet* and *Othello*, Ophelia and Desdemona, does not save them from untimely and violent deaths. Prince Hal rids himself of the degrading presence of Falstaff without a qualm, telling him to his face, "I know thee not, old man."* Just as King Lear and his estranged daughter Cordelia are reunited and looking forward to making up their differences, she is murdered. All of Shakespeare's many characters are imagined with penetrating empathy. But none is immune to the hazards of mortal life in a harsh world.

Resolution and Meaning

> The chief pitfall threatening any discussion
> of Shakespeare's thought is the common
> assumption that the opinions of any character
> in a Shakespearean play are Shakespeare's own.
> Shakespeare was not a propagandist; he did not
> write plays as vehicles for his own ideas. Rather
> he developed a theatre of dialectical conflict, in
> which idea is pitted against idea and from their
> friction a deeper understanding of the issues
> emerges. The resolution which is reached is
> not the negation of conflict, but the stasis
> produced by art.
>
> —Germaine Greer, *Shakespeare*

Resolution and meaning in contemporary drama tend to focus on the fate of individuals, either in the context of a family or in isolation. If we apply contemporary practice to the plays of Shakespeare and confine our search for meaning to an appreciation of his most interesting characters, however, we may overlook other things that the plays have to offer. Fascinating as Hamlet, Macbeth, and Othello may be, the plays in which they appear are intended as more than personality studies.

Shakespeare and his fellow Elizabethans inherited much of their dramatic method from the theatre of the Middle Ages. In the medieval tradition, a cycle of many short plays based on the books of the Bible was performed in the course of several days or weeks at prescribed times of the year. Because the Bible presents the history of the world from the Creation to Judgment Day, the effect of this marathon performance was to give the audience a picture of the total life of humanity in the context of eternity.

Shakespeare, too, offers a picture of a complete human world in each of his plays. In order to achieve this many-sided image of humanity, he creates complicated dramatic structures. Through the use of intricate plots, he shows us the conflict from contrasting angles. His cast of characters is large and covers the full spectrum of human types, from clowns to kings, each of whom, from the highest to the lowest, is alive with projects, purposes, and objectives.

*It is said that Queen Elizabeth liked the "fat knight" so much that she ordered Shakespeare to bring him back in *The Merry Wives of Windsor*.

In his resolutions, Shakespeare brings all of these forces into balance, giving the audience a final image of the whole world of the play.

But this balance, as Germaine Greer points out, does not represent Shakespeare's personal conclusions on the issues—ambition, jealousy, conscience, romantic love, or the divine authority of kings,—with which the play deals. Instead, Shakespeare lets the play speak for all sides of an issue, and in the resolution he invites us to put together our own picture of humanness by combining his images of action with our responses. If in our reading we approach the resolution in this way, we can play the same role as the Globe audience did when they heard Shakespeare's plays in performance. The following checklist contains some specific questions which may help the beginning reader assemble the many aspects of a Shakespeare play into a complete pattern.

A Checklist
READING SHAKESPEARE

- *Who's there and where are they?*
  Because Shakespeare wrote for a versatile and complex performance space, his scripts contain many different kinds of dramatic space. Although the stage is, of course, always the same size, the scope of the action varies widely. In soliloquies, all attention is focused on a single character, as in a movie close-up. Other scenes are like the medium shot, with two or three characters dominating the space. The panoramic scenes (long shots), such as the play-within-the-play in *Hamlet,* and the many scenes of battle or final resolution may be imagined as using the whole stage, with twenty or more actors in the dramatic space. Notice how, in the sequence of scenes, the scope of the dramatic space changes.

- *Does the character seem to be inside or outside the action, or both?*
  Shakespearean characters frequently seem to stand back from the action and comment on it as if they were in the audience. Although it may seem artificial to readers of realistic drama, this conduct is, in fact, a common form of human behavior. We can observe it in ourselves when we are absorbed in a difficult task or in the grip of a strong feeling but self-aware at the same time. If we were able to fully articulate this self-awareness to a group of people watching us, we would be doing what Shakespeare's characters often do.

- *Who is the instigator of the action and who is the agent?*
  An instigator is a character with a clear objective who wants a character other than himself (the agent) to overcome an obstacle. Part of the obstacle may be the agent's unwillingness to take action. Eventually the agent agrees, or pretends to, and goes along with the instigator's objective. Often the agent is divided within himself about the objective but pursues it anyway. This complex pattern of conflict is at the heart of most of Shakespeare's plots. Further complexities arise when the agent employs subagents or when the instigator's stated objective is different from his hidden objective, which may be to destroy the agent himself.

- *What opposing views of human behavior are dramatized?*
  Shakespeare usually presents human thought and action from contrasting viewpoints. In *Hamlet,* for instance, Hamlet pretends to be mad, but Ophelia becomes truly mad; Hamlet considers, and then rejects, suicide, but Ophelia drowns herself; Ophelia pretends to pray, but Claudius tries to pray in earnest; Hamlet, Laertes, and Fortinbras all seek to revenge their fathers' deaths in different ways; Hamlet, Claudius, the Queen, and Laertes all suffer, in different ways, from a guilty conscience. Most of Shakespeare's plays contain recurrent types of behavior presented in changing perspectives.

12 ❧ Comedy of Manners

*The art of comedy is an undeceiving, an
emancipation from error, an unmasking.*
—Eric Bentley
Drama Critic

One of the most enduring traditions in drama is the comedy of manners. Begun in ancient Greece, it was adapted by the Romans, admired in medieval cloisters and Renaissance centers of higher learning, and flourished in the indoor theatres of seventeenth- and eighteenth-century London and Paris. The first important American drama, Royall Tyler's *The Contrast,* of 1787, was a comedy of manners. In the modern era the tradition was further developed by Bernard Shaw, Oscar Wilde, and Noel Coward. Elements of the comedy of manners are still with us today in the work of Neil Simon and in television situation comedy.

Comedy of manners, the drama of social behavior, is meant to keep us civilized by making us laugh at our antisocial tendencies. It is also, in its fullest form, a drama which celebrates social continuity and renewal, affirms the succession of youth to social power, and reminds us that good sense is more fun in the long run than extremism and crankiness. It is this spirit which keeps the plays of Molière, Oliver Goldsmith, and Richard Brinsley Sheridan alive for today's readers and playgoers alike.

Many comedies of manners were written during the seventeenth and eighteenth centuries. But the most universally applauded came from the pen of French actor-manager Jean Baptiste Poquelin de Molière. Under the patronage of Louis XIV, Molière wrote, produced, and acted in dozens of comic masterpieces before his death in 1673, including *The School for Wives, Tartuffe, The Misanthrope, The Miser,* and *The Imaginary Invalid.*

When Charles II was restored to the English throne in 1660, he brought with him a taste for comedy of manners which he had acquired during his exile in France. Encouraged by the king and influenced by Molière, English dramatists such as William Congreve, William Wycherley, George Etherege, and George Farquhar created a brilliant body of drama now known as Restoration Comedy, in recognition of the return of Charles II. Wycherley even adapted one of Molière's plays, *The Misanthrope,* for the English stage, calling it *The Plain Dealer.* Restoration comedy, however, disappeared with its aristocratic audience. The rising middle class made its presence felt in early eighteenth-century theatre, and a new form—sentimental, or tearful, comedy—held the stage. In the late 1700's Goldsmith and Sheridan tried to bring back the spirit of the Restoration by making comedy less tearful and more funny. Three of their plays—*She Stoops to Conquer, The Rivals,* and *The School for Scandal*—have enjoyed steady popularity since the time of the American Revolution.

In eighteenth-century France, comedies of manners continued to be written by such authors as Marivaux and Beaumarchais, whose *Marriage of Figaro* inspired Mozart's opera of the same name—and, some say, the French Revolution. Goldoni in Italy and Holberg in Denmark also wrote in this tradition.

An appreciation of comedy of manners begins with an understanding of the theatres the authors wrote for. Although important differences exist between the aristocratic theatres of the seventeenth century and the larger, more democratic playhouses of the eighteenth, they also have much in common. In the following section we emphasize these common qualities and see how they shed light on selected moments from two typical comedies of manners: Molière's *Tartuffe* and Sheridan's *School for Scandal.*

The Comedy-of-Manners Playhouse

At first glance, a playhouse of seventeenth- or eighteenth-century London or Paris might look like one of our own proscenium theatres. But as the audience gathers and the performance begins, we notice important differences. For one thing there are usually three distinct seating areas corresponding to the social class to which the ticket holder happens to belong. If we are middle class, we sit on benches or chairs in the pit (today's orchestra) from where we can see the upper classes in the rows of boxes which line the side walls of the auditorium; these boxes face one another, affording an overall view of both the stage and the auditorium. Servants and members of the working class are seated behind and above in the gallery (balcony). The auditorium remains lit during the performance and these three groups can watch one another as well as the actors. These audiences go to the theatre to see and be seen socially as well as to see and hear the play. This does not mean, however, that they are inattentive. Like the crowds at a modern sporting event, they can socialize and pay close attention to the game at the same time. The subject of the comedy is social behavior—manners—and the playhouse itself offers a continuing view of the real people whose manners are mirrored in the drama.

In *Tartuffe* (Script 12) the setting throughout is "Orgon's house in Paris." The role of the audience is to imagine what kind of house it is and in what kinds of rooms the action takes place. A table is all that is required for the climactic moment in which the dupe, Orgon, finally catches on to Tartuffe, the con man. But, although Orgon is under the table, the fun of the scene is that he is visible to the audience—just as he is when he hides behind his wife, Elmire. The script implies a kind of game in which characters become "invisible," not in reality but by convention. Since actor and spectator are visible to one another in the candlelight, the game is shared by all as a part of the larger game of dramatic and social impersonation.

Script 12

From Molière's
Tartuffe (translated by Richard Wilbur).

Who's there? Orgon, his wife, Elmire, and Tartuffe.
Setting. Orgon's house in Paris.
Occasion. Tartuffe is expecting to receive sexual favors from Elmire.
Situation. Elmire has hidden her husband, Orgon, under the table to
   prove to him that Tartuffe is a scoundrel.

[*Act IV, scene 5.* TARTUFFE, ELMIRE, ORGON (*under the table*).]
   TARTUFFE: Why worry about the man? Each day he grows/ More
      gullible; one can lead him by the nose.
   ELMIRE: Nevertheless, do step out for a minute/ Into the hall and see
      that no one's in it.

[*Scene 6.* ORGON, ELMIRE.]
   ORGON [*coming out from under the table*]: The man's a perfect
      monster, I must admit./ I'm simply stunned, I can't get over it.
   ELMIRE: What, coming out so soon? How premature!/ Get back in
      hiding and wait until you're sure./ Stay till the end, and be
      convinced completely;/ We mustn't stop till things are proved
      concretely.
   ORGON: Hell never harbored anything so vicious!
   ELMIRE: Tut, don't be hasty. Try to be judicious./ Wait, and be certain
      there's no mistake./ No jumping to conclusions, for Heaven's sake!
[*She places* ORGON *behind her, as* TARTUFFE *reenters.*]
[*Scene 7.* TARTUFFE, ELMIRE, ORGON.]
   TARTUFFE [*not seeing* ORGON]: Madam, all things have worked out to
      perfection;/ I've given the neighboring rooms a full inspection;/ No
      one's about , and now I may, at last—
   ORGON [*intercepting him*]: Hold on my passionate fellow, not so fast!

   Notice that the stage directions indicate three scenes. In all, the script
of *Tartuffe* contains thirty-one such divisions. This does not mean that
the play starts and stops thirty-one times, however. Used in many
classical scripts, these scene divisions merely signal the arrival or de-
parture of one or more characters, replacing the more familiar "exit"
and "enter" designations. The action of *Tartuffe* is continuous. "Scene 6.
ORGON and ELMIRE" tells us that Tartuffe has left the stage. When he
returns his name reappears in the script, making it "scene 7." This is
the *french scene* method and can help the reader imagine dramatic
space, since every change in "who's there?" is recorded. In the modern
theatre, many stage managers use the french scene method to organize
rehearsals.

Simultaneous behavior in Script 12 is intricate. Elmire has put her husband under the table to trap Tartuffe into revealing his secret lust for her. The reader can imagine both Orgon's reaction to Tartuffe's advances and the audience's reaction to Orgon. In comedy of manners, the characters seem to inhabit a setting which is partly within the fictional world of the action and partly in the world of the audience. When we imagine dramatic space in these scripts, we should include both theatre and audience.

Script 13 is an excerpt from *The School for Scandal*, first performed in London in 1777. Although the basic elements of dramatic space—setting and simultaneous behavior—are as important as ever, they function differently here than in the modern script.

The setting is Joseph Surface's library. But the audience does not expect, nor does the theatre produce, the kind of detailed setting we would see at a performance of *A Raisin in the Sun* or *Arms and the Man*. In fact, what the audience probably saw was a familiar painted backdrop used in any production which required a library scene. The function of the scenery was to provide a general indication of setting, not an elaborate environment. Only the most necessary furniture was used, and actors tended to stay downstage of the scenery in order to avoid clashing with the artificial dimensions of the painted canvas. The actor was expected to maintain visual dominance and contact with the audience, not to "live" in the setting. The physical presence of the actor was what created the theatrical event. All else was there to enhance this presence.

Although the audience no longer sat on the stage in 1777, they did occupy proscenium boxes directly adjacent to the acting area. When Sir Peter speaks "aside" he may very well be addressing spectators within several feet of where he stands. It is not out of the question to imagine these spectators urging him to tell Charles his secret—that there is a lady behind the screen. The fun is that these spectators know what Sir Peter does not; the lady is his own wife. A famous engraving of the period depicts the moment just after Charles "throws down the screen," revealing Lady Teazle. In this picture, one of the characters, probably Sir Peter, is shown in conventional "aside' posture—head turned toward the audience, hand hiding face from the other characters. This posture makes him "inaudible" in the same way that Orgon, in Script 12, is "invisible." Although not indicated in the script, he can be imagined sharing with the public his discovery: "Lady Teazle, by all that's damnable!" In any case, an important part of the simultaneous behavior in this scene is a direct appeal for audience participation. The question "where are they?" actually has two answers. In terms of dramatic space they are in Joseph Surface's library, as the script tells us. In terms of the theatre event, they are on the playhouse stage, where Sir Peter shares a secret with the audience and the audience share a bigger secret with one another.

Script 13 is compounded of asides, whispers, screens, and closets, reflecting the audience's interest in masks, disguises, and whisperings of their own. Places of intrigue and titillation, playhouses were showcases of the latest styles of behavior. The conspirational hushing between Charles and Sir Peter is

Script 13

From Richard Brinsley Sheridan's
The School for Scandal.

Who's there? Charles Surface and Sir Peter Teazle. Charles' brother, Joseph, enters later.

Setting. In the library of Joseph's home.

Occasion. The two men are discussing Joseph's character. Sir Peter intends to prove that Joseph is not as stuffy as Charles thinks he is by revealing that he has hidden a woman in the room.

Situation. Unknown to Sir Peter, the woman behind the screen is actually Lady Teazle, Sir Peter's wife.

SIR PETER: Ah, Charles, if you associated more with your brother, one might indeed hope for your reformation. He is a man of sentiment. Well, there is nothing in the world so noble as a man of sentiment.

CHARLES: Pshaw! He is too moral by half, and so apprehensive of his good name, as he calls it, that I suppose he would as soon let a priest into his house as a girl.

SIR PETER: No, no,—come, come,—you wrong him. No, no, Joseph is no rake, but he is no such saint in that respect either. [*Aside.*] I have a great mind to tell him—we should have a laugh.

CHARLES: Oh hang him! He's a very anchorite, a young hermit!

SIR PETER: Hark'ee—you must not abuse him: he may chance to hear of it again, I promise you.

CHARLES: Why, you won't tell him?

SIR PETER: No—but this way. [*Aside.*] Egad, I'll tell him. Hark'ee, have you a mind to have a good laugh at Joseph!

CHARLES: I should like it of all things.

SIR PETER: Then, i'faith, we will! [*Whispers.*] I'll be quit with him for discovering me. He had a girl with him when I called.

CHARLES: What! Joseph? You jest.

SIR PETER: Hush!—a little French milliner—and the best of the jest is—she's in the room now.

CHARLES [*looking at the closet*]: The Devil she is!

SIR PETER [*points to the screen*]: Hush! I tell you.

CHARLES: Behind the screen! Odds life, let's unveil her!

SIR PETER: No, no—he's coming—you shan't indeed!

CHARLES: Oh, egad, we'll have a peep at the little milliner!

SIR PETER: Not for the world! Joseph will never forgive me.

CHARLES: I'll stand by you—

SIR PETER: Odds, here he is!

[JOSEPH SURFACE *enters just as* CHARLES SURFACE *throws down the screen.*]

CHARLES: Lady Teazle, by all that's wonderful!

SIR PETER: Lady Teazle, by all that's damnable!

CHARLES: Sir Peter, this is one of the smartest French milliners I ever saw.

✿ *Theatregoing in Seventeenth-Century Paris*

In the following excerpt from the opening scene of *Cyrano de Bergerac,* written in 1897, Edmond Rostand dramatizes seventeenth-century play-going. The Hotel de Bourgogne (Burgundy Hall) did, in fact, exist in 1640, and it housed the rivals of Molière's Troupe du Monsieur. The script distinguishes two auditorium areas, the pit and the boxes. The pit (also "parterre," "plateaux," "place," or "yard," depending on the period) is the main floor. Here the audience stands or sits on benches or chairs. It is the most public part of the auditorium. For refined persons and ladies (not always the same thing) who required more privacy, there were boxes lining the walls on a second level. The stage itself was also used by the more daring patrons. As this type of playhouse evolved and enlarged, a third area—the gallery—was installed at an upper level in the rear of the hall. These were the cheapest seats, inhabited by the serving and working classes, who came to be known, by their imperious manners, as "the gods." Note that the Lamplighter lights the auditorium chandeliers so that the audience can see one another. These auditorium chandeliers remain lit during the performance.

From Edmond Rostand's
Cyrano de Bergerac (English version by David Scanlan).

[*The Hotel de Bourgogne, Paris, 1640. An indoor tennis court adapted for use as a theatre. . . . The audience gradually arrives:* Cavaliers, Citizens, Lackeys, Page, *a* Pickpocket, *the* Doorkeepers, *etc. Then the* Fops, *a* Waitress *with refreshments, members of the orchestra, etc.*]

---

contagious. The audience, in its turn, is in conspiracy against the characters' ignorance of the true situation. The "good" brother, Joseph, has hidden Sir Peter's wife behind his library screen, for purposes of his own. What is more, there might be persons in the theatre at this moment who might be suspected of similar behavior in real life. How can we resist stealing a glance in their direction to see the look on their faces when Lady Teazle is revealed? Eighteenth-century London was a small city by our standards, and the theatregoing circle were largely known to one another. The actors in *The School for Scandal* presented themselves in dress, language, and manner as typical Londoners of the day.

Prose and Verse

The characters in a typical comedy of manners say everything they think and feel in a clear and orderly way. This may not be a realistic way of talking, but it is an effective way of making real thoughts and feelings clear to the audience.

FOP [*seeing the hall is not yet full*]: What? Have we made our entrance like tailors? No one to disturb, no toes to step on? [*Recognizes other noblemen.*] Cuigy! Bressaille! [*General embracing.*]

CUIGY: Faithful comrades! Yes, we're here before they've even lit the candles.

FOP: Infuriating!

ANOTHER FOP: Take heart, Marquis, here comes the lamplighter.

ENTIRE AUDIENCE [*hailing the entrance of the* Lamplighter]: Hurrah, hurrah! [*They crowd around the chandeliers as he lights them.*]

CUIGY [*from the pit*]: Quite a crowd.

CHRISTIAN: Quite.

FOP: All the smart set.

[*The* Fops *identify various elegantly turned-out* Ladies *entering the boxes above. Exchanges of bows and smiles. Three taps on the stage announce the rise of the curtain. Everyone is silent with expectation. From behind the curtain a* Fop's *voice is heard.*]

FOP [*off*]: Watch that candle!

ANOTHER FOP [*poking his head through the curtain*]: A chair!

[*A chair is passed over the heads of the audience. The* Fop *takes it, throws several kisses up to the boxes, and disappears behind the curtain.*]

SPECTATOR: Silence!

[*The three knocks are repeated. The curtain opens. Several* Fops *sit at the sides of the stage in impudent poses. The blue backdrop tells us the play is a "pastoral." Four little crystal chandeliers light the stage. The violinists play softly.*]

And this was, after all, the dramatist's objective. As the eighteenth-century author Samuel Johnson put it:

The drama's laws the drama's patrons give,*
And we who live to please must please to live.

Dr. Johnson chose rhymed verse to express this sentiment because of the formality of the occasion for which it was written—the opening of the Drury Lane Theatre. But he was, like many playwrights of his time, a master of English prose as well.

In *Tartuffe* and *The School for Scandal* we have examples of a comedy in verse and a comedy in prose.

Molière wrote some of his plays in prose and others in verse. This gave his actors two different "voices" to act in. The difference between prose and verse

*That is, in drama, we the audience make the laws.

in performance is a bit like the difference between talking and singing. While talking is more natural and informal, singing is more intense. The choice of verse or prose is an important element in setting the basic atmosphere of a play. But, unless you read French, you may never know for sure whether the Molière play you're reading was written in verse or not, since many translators use prose for all his plays. Luckily for those readers who want to get as close as they can to the original, three of Molière's greatest plays—*The School for Wives, The Misanthrope,* and *Tartuffe*—have been brilliantly translated into English verse by the poet Richard Wilbur.

The dialogue in Script 12 gives us an example of Wilbur's translation of Molière's dialogue into iambic pentameter. This means, as in Shakespeare, that a typical line will have ten syllables and five stresses. The stress usually comes on the second, fourth, sixth, eighth, and last syllables. When interpreted by a skilled reader, iambic pentameter does not have a singsong sound. Instead, the rhythmic pattern provides a subtle background beat to the conversational flow. The same is true of the rhymes. In reading this dialogue aloud, let the natural inflections of the lines stand out, and keep the rhyme in the background. The most important thing is to make empathic connection with the thoughts and feelings of the characters. The verse will then act as a lens that brings the dramatic behavior into sharper focus.

The dialogue in *School for Scandal* may sound artificial to our modern ears but it is not far from the spoken English of its day. One of the problems in reading the theatre dialogue of Sheridan, Goldsmith, and other dramatists of this period is in the punctuation. If you are in the habit of trying to pronounce punctuation, such a script will present insurmountable difficulties. It may be better to ignore the punctuation and let the flow of ideas and feelings take over, as they do in real conversation. It's also a good idea not to let old-fashioned slang like "odds life," "i'faith," "egad," and "pshaw" get in the way. If we make contact with the underlying feelings, we will hear the characters' humanity more clearly.

Conflict and Recognition

Molière's method of presenting conflict often resembles the method found in the episodes of Greek tragedy. Most of the french scenes that make up *Tartuffe*, for example, contain direct, one-on-one conflicts that drive the action forward in a steady and unwavering direction. Like his settings, Molière's dramatic action is stripped down to essentials. The reader of *Tartuffe* will experience a sequence of conflicts that is both logical and swift.

The play opens with a family dispute. Five members of Orgon's family are trying to persuade his mother, Mme Pernelle, to get rid of Tartuffe, an overbearing hypocrite whom Orgon has taken into the household. Orgon **wants** to make him the family saint, **but** the family regard him as a disruptive and dangerous nuisance. Mme Pernelle takes Orgon's side against the family in the first scene. In the following several scenes we see Orgon himself in conflict with a succession of family members who are struggling against the tyranny of Tartuffe's presence.

In the next phase of the action, Orgon's daughter, Mariane, has a fight with her lover, Valère, because she is unable to defy her father's wish that she marry Tartuffe. This conflict is resolved by the servant Dorine. But Orgon's obsession with Tartuffe remains the obstacle to complete family harmony. (In the society of that time, Orgon's insistence that his daughter marry the man of his choice had almost the force of law.)

When Tartuffe is introduced, he turns out to be even worse than the family had feared. First he clashes with Dorine, whose neckline he pretends to find immodest. He then attempts to seduce Orgon's wife, Elmire, but she resists his advances. Damis, Orgon's son, witnesses the attempted seduction from a closet, calls his father, and exposes Tartuffe's rascally behavior. But Orgon is so moved by Tartuffe's fake humility that he disinherits Damis instead. Orgon and Tartuffe then join forces against the whole family.

After sixteen french scenes, a pattern of three macroconflicts has emerged, each more intense than the last: the family vs. Mme Pernelle, the family vs. Orgon, and Orgon and Tartuffe taking the offensive against the family. At this point Orgon, speaking to Tartuffe, reveals his underlying objective:

> It pleases me to vex them, and for spite
> What's more, I'm going to drive them to despair
> By making you my only son and heir.

What defense can the family offer against such tyranny? Cléante, Orgon's brother-in-law, tries to reason with Tartuffe. Elmire and Mariane appeal to Orgon's feelings. Neither tactic works. Finally, Elmire devises a plan to offer proof: Orgon must hide under a table and see with his own eyes how his pious hero behaves when alone with his wife. The first major moment of recognition occurs in Act IV, scenes 6 and 7 (Script 12), when Orgon must face the unpleasant truth: Tartuffe does really mean to seduce Elmire. This recognition reverses the terms of the conflict. Now Orgon **wants** Tartuffe out of his house, **but** the house belongs to Tartuffe, whom Orgon made his heir when he disinherited Damis:

> ORGON: Spare me your falsehoods and get out of here.
> TARTUFFE: No, I'm the master, and you're the one to go!

Orgon now must face not only the truth of Tartuffe's real nature but the consequences of his own monstrous gullibility and arrogance as well. In the remaining scenes of the play, the family fight a losing battle against Tartuffe's takeover until, in a *deus ex machina* ending, an officer from the king comes to arrest Tartuffe, and the conflict is miraculously resolved.

Like most English comedies of the eighteenth century, Sheridan's *The Rivals* has a more elaborate pattern of conflicts than is usually found in

Molière. As the title suggests, there are a number of male rivals for the hands of a number of women. Each love story has its own conflict, and each is interwoven with the others. In the foreground of the action are the principal lovers, Capt. Jack Absolute and Miss Lydia Languish. Jack **wants** to marry Lydia, **but** Lydia is a romantic and wants to elope with a mysterious stranger, like the heroines of the novels she constantly reads. Knowing this, Jack decides to call himself "Ensign Beverly" and woo Lydia in disguise. "For though I am convinced my little Lydia would elope with me as Ensign Beverly," he tells a friend, "yet I am by no means certain that she would take me with the impediment of our friends' consent, a regular humdrum wedding, and the reversion of a good fortune on my side." Meanwhile, Jack's father, Sir Anthony, **wants** to arrange a marriage between Jack and Lydia, **but** Lydia is in love with Ensign Beverly and rejects the proposal. This means that Jack is his own rival. Pursuing his objective with vigor, Sir Anthony orders his son to propose to Lydia personally. When he forces Jack to see her, Lydia is amazed to find herself, or so she thinks, in the presence of her beloved Beverly. A moment of truth is at hand. "Come here, sirrah," Sir Anthony says to Jack. "Who the devil are you?" This moment of recognition reverses the lovers' relationship and creates a new conflict. Lydia is enraged at both the deception and the prospect of a conventional wedding instead of a romantic elopement. She rejects both Beverly and Jack and sweeps out of the room. Only when Jack risks his life in a duel with another false rival does Lydia's heart soften, as love, at long last, conquers all.

Plot and Character

The plot of *The Rivals* is, of course, the traditional comedy-of-manners plot in which all conflict is resolved in the final union of the lovers—in this case, four pairs of them. An unusual twist, however, is Sheridan's choice of obstacle in the main conflict. In most comedies a cranky or fanatical member of the older generation stands in the way of true love. In *Tartuffe,* for instance, Orgon's devotion to his hypocritical idol and his underlying obsession with paternal power keep Mariane and Valère apart. But in *The Rivals*, Lydia herself—or, more precisely, Lydia's obsession with romance—creates the obstacle to her marriage to Jack. The elders, Sir Anthony and Mrs. Malaprop, Lydia's aunt, are actually striving to bring about the marriage. Sir Anthony, Mrs. Malaprop, and Jack himself **want** Lydia to marry Jack, **but** Lydia wants to elope with a fantasy. Her obsession with this fantasy is finally cured by the real possibility that Jack will be killed in a duel.

   The comic plot has two basic variations. In such plays as *The Importance of Being Earnest, Arms and the Man,* and *The Rivals,* one of the lovers is the protagonist, and the love story occupies the foreground of the action. In another variation, the love story is kept in the background, and the protagonist is that member of the older generation whose obsessive behavior or "humour" gets in the way. While the marriage of Mariane and Valère is an important

❧   *Comedy of Humours*

In the time of Shakespeare, characters whose behavior was especially pretentious or obsessive were thought of as "humour" characters. Playwright Ben Jonson specialized in such characters and created a kind of drama called comedy of humours. He peopled such plays as *Volpone* and *The Alchemist* with characters whose behavior in all circumstances flowed from one particular quality, such as piety, sensuality, pride, or greed. The humours concept was based on a medieval theory of medicine which linked individual behavior with four *humours,* or bodily fluids. Black bile, it was held, made a person melancholy; yellow bile produced anger; blood was the cause of passion and good cheer; and phlegm was the source of calm or apathy. Although the term *humour* is associated primarily with this theory and with Jonson's adaptation of it to drama, this approach to characterization can be found throughout the history of comedy. "Humours" are clearly a major source of the humor which makes us laugh at certain kinds of obsessive behavior, whatever the historical period.

---

aspect of the situation in *Tartuffe,* Orgon is the protagonist, and so the play centers on the working out of his objectives. This is also the case in Molière's *The Miser,* in which the protagonist is Harpagon, a money-mad father who stands in the way of the marriages of both his son and daughter. Comedies of the first kind will give the reader a picture of society in general, while the second type offers an investigation of a particular antisocial obsession.

Because the goal of the comedy of manners was to mirror the nature of society, antisocial behavior is always the obstacle to social or personal harmony. The obsession which produces this behavior may be an obstacle to the lovers' objectives, as in the case of Lydia Languish, or it may be an obstacle to the character's personal objectives, as in the case of Mrs. Malaprop. Mrs. Malaprop, a lonely widow who is particularly proud of her supposed command of the English language, **wants** to attract male attention by displays of intellect, **but** she defeats herself every time she opens her mouth:

MRS. MALAPROP: There, sir, an attack upon my language! what do you think of that?—an aspersion upon my parts of speech! Was ever such a brute! Sure, if I reprehend any thing in this world it is the use of my oracular tongue, and a nice derangement of epitaphs.

By using "reprehend" for "comprehend," "oracular" for "vernacular," "derangement" for "arrangement," and "epitaphs" for "epithets"—and all in one sentence—Mrs. Malaprop dramatizes the absurdity, not only of her own affectations, but of those in the audience who try to impress others with their use of words. What Lydia, Mrs. Malaprop, and the audience learn is that people are loved, not for their pretensions, but for themselves.

These pretensions or obsessions are often suggested in the character's name. Lydia languishes over her fantasies. Mrs. Malaprop's choice of words is so wildly inappropriate (malapropos) that a new English word, *malapropism*, was coined in recognition of her talent for erroneous speech. The cast list of *The Rivals* contains other such names. Sir Anthony Absolute is absolutely sure he is always right and will get his own way, absolutely. Sir Lucius O'Trigger likes to settle all disputes with dueling pistols. Bob Acres, a rural fellow, is incorrigibly earthy. A century earlier, Restoration comedy cast lists included such expressive names as Pinchwife, Squeamish, Fainall, Foible, Mincing, and Lady Bountiful. Obviously, these are not intended to be taken as real names. They are used more in the spirit of the nicknames we give to friends who seem to be forever repeating the same behavior. The intention was the same then as it is now: to humanize one another through laughter.

Resolution and Meaning

Much of the fun of comedy comes from unmasking an impostor. A young man who is Ernest in town and Jack in the country is found out (*The Importance of Being Earnest*). A young woman who imposes her romantic airs on everyone meets a man who calls her a liar (*Arms and the Man*). A man who pretends to the highest virtues is actually hiding another man's wife behind a screen (*The School for Scandal*). Sooner or later, in comedy, the screen comes tumbling down, the truth comes out, and everyone lives happily ever after.

Impostor characters act in several different ways. In one kind of action they pretend to be something they are not in order to get what they want. Tartuffe, for instance, wants power over Orgon's family and property. Because he knows that Orgon is gullible when it comes to religion he pretends to be a very pious person. In William Wycherley's *The Country Wife*, Mr. Horner pretends to be a eunuch so that all the husbands will leave him alone with their wives. These characters' antisocial objectives are not revealed until they are forcefully unmasked.

But not all imposture serves antisocial ends. Pretense must frequently be resorted to in order to unite the young lovers. This is why Jack Absolute pretends to be Beverly. Similarly, in Goldsmith's *She Stoops to Conquer*, Miss Hardcastle pretends to be a barmaid to help break the ice with her would-be lover, who is terrified of women of his own class. When the objective is achieved, this kind of pretender willingly throws off the disguise and claims the prize.

The action of the humour character is also a kind of imposture. But, unlike characters who only use pretense to get what they want, humour characters believe in their pretensions and demand that others do likewise. Lacking the self-awareness of either the villainous or heroic pretender, the humour character's action turns out to be self-defeating. Orgon, in the process of

❦ *Comedy and Laughter*

Drama is often symbolized by a pair of masks, one laughing, the other weeping. The weeping mask represents Melpomene, the Muse of tragedy, and the laughing mask symbolizes the Muse of comedy, Thalia. This symbol reminds us that comedy and laughter are inseparable. Where does laughter come from? There is no easy answer to this question. The twin Muses, however, bring to mind an old French proverb: He who feels, weeps; he who thinks, laughs. Our response to drama, as we have seen, has both feeling and thinking aspects. It may be that comedy makes us laugh by triggering the thinking aspect. Another explanation was put forward by the French philosopher Henri Bergson who said that laughter is caused by mechanical behavior. An example of this idea can be found in Act I, scene 4 of Molière's *Tartuffe*. Orgon, the head of the family, is obsessed with the well-being of his house guest and idol, Tartuffe. When he returns home after a short absence, he greets all family news with the same mechanical response, "And Tartuffe?" and all news of Tartuffe with, "Poor fellow!" English playwright Christopher Fry wrote that laughter "is surely the surest touch of genius in Creation."

---

proving to his family that he is all powerful, gives away what power he has to Tartuffe. Lydia Languish nearly loses her lover by insisting on her romantic fantasies. Mrs. Malaprop makes a fool of herself with the very behavior she thinks will bring her love and admiration. Such characters become lovable and admirable only after they drop their pretensions and behave like human beings.

Traditional comedy invariably ends with all of the characters onstage and all pretense at an end. The antisocial impostors have been unmasked and their objectives thwarted, the deceptions and disguises of the lovers have been joyfully cast off, and the humour characters are cured of their obsessions and happily accept a society which is renewed by the energies of youth. Characters who cannot or will not relinquish their humours face social exile, as does Alceste in *The Misanthrope*, or even madness—Harpagon's obsession with money, in *The Miser*, goes beyond a pretense to power when he apprehends himself as the thief who stole his money box. The values of a renewed society—sanity, prosperity, love, and a hopeful vision of the future—require that all characters drop their pretenses and embrace their true condition. In the epilogue to *The School for Scandal*, Lady Teazle, the woman behind the screen, includes the audience in the dramatic space as she advises us to follow her example:

Blessed were the fair like [me], her faults who stopped,
And closed her follies when the curtain dropped!
No more in vice and error to engage,
Or play the fool on life's great stage.

A Checklist

READING COMEDY OF MANNERS

- *Does the script indicate the presence of an audience?*
  Pay particular attention to prologues, asides, and epilogues, in which characters speak directly to the audience. They are forceful reminders of the participatory nature of the comedy-of-manners theatre event. Playing the audience's role, the reader is constantly invited to participate in as well as to judge the dramatic action.

- *Who is the protagonist?*
  The protagonist is either one of the young lovers, or a member of the older generation who represents an obstacle to young love. Identifying this character brings the reader to the heart of the conflict.

- *What "humours" are dramatized?*
  The purpose of the comedy of manners is to present character from the perspective of social behavior, not personal psychology. To achieve clarity of focus, only one aspect of the character's behavior—sometimes called his "humour"—is usually dramatized. It is the effect of this humour on social interaction, rather than its underlying causes, that is the subject of comedy of manners. Do the humours of these plays still exist in today's society?

- *Which characters are fooling others, which are fooled by others, and which are fooling themselves?*
  Comedy asks us to see ourselves as others see us. In the midst of all the foolery, self-aware readers will recognize aspects of their own social behavior. By recognizing and enjoying foolishness when we see it, we may even learn how not to be fooled—by ourselves or others.

Part Four

MODERN DRAMA
Images of Action
Artfully Assembled
in an Individualized
Mise en Scène

13 ❧ Introduction to Modern Drama

SOLNESS: I don't build church towers anymore.
  Or churches either.
HILDA: Then what do you build?
SOLNESS: Homes for human beings.
  —Henrik Ibsen, *The Master Builder*

Life on the stage should be as it really is,
and the people, too, should be as they are, not
on stilts.
  —Anton Chekhov

MACHEATH: What do you mean, nice? That isn't
  nice, you idiot, that's art, and art
  isn't nice!
  —Bertolt Brecht, *The Threepenny Opera*

Modern drama began as a rebellion against the idealism and romanticism of the nineteenth-century stage, which presented images of life as it should be. The founders of modern drama wanted to present life as it is.

Life As It Is

This movement was international in scope. After writing verse dramas on historical subjects for a quarter of a century, Norwegian poet Henrik Ibsen devoted the remaining decades of his career to the creation of realistic plays about the problems of ordinary people. London-based Irish novelist and critic George Bernard Shaw, an Ibsen admirer, declared war on the idealists of the English stage (including Shakespeare) and extolled the superiority of the "masters of reality." In Russia, Anton Chekhov joined forces with the actors of the Moscow Art Theatre to create a drama which explored the richness and mystery of everyday life. And in the United States, Eugene O'Neill rebelled against the melodramatics of his actor-father by putting common sailors and dirt farmers on the stage instead of the French counts and biblical patriarchs favored by the great James O'Neill.

❧ Idealistic and Realistic Views of Military Action

From Alfred Lord Tennyson's poem *The Charge of the Light Brigade* (1854).

I

Half a league, half a league,
Half a league onward.
All in the valley of Death
 Rode the six hundred.
"Forward the Light Brigade!
Charge for the guns!" he said.
Into the valley of Death
 Rode the six hundred. . . .

VI

When can their glory fade?
O the wild charge they made!
 All the world wonder'd.
Honor the charge they made!
Honor the Light Brigade,
 Noble six hundred!

From Act I of George Bernard Shaw's
Arms and the Man (1894).

THE MAN: You never saw a cavalry charge, did you?

RAINA: How could I?

THE MAN: Ah, perhaps not—of course. Well, it's a funny sight. It's like slinging a handful of peas against a window pane: first one comes; then two or three close behind him; and then all the rest in a lump.

RAINA [*her eyes dilating as she raises her clasped hands ecstatically*]: Yes, the first One!—the bravest of the brave!

THE MAN [*prosaically*]: Hm! You should see the poor devil pulling at his horse.

RAINA: Why should he pull at his horse?

THE MAN [*impatient at so stupid a question*]: It's running away with him of course: do you suppose the fellow wants to get there before the others and be killed?

In addition to rebelling against idealism, modern drama is in continuing revolt against itself. August Strindberg rejected the realism of surfaces by offering a vision of life as it is, seen from the inside. The dramas of Luigi Pirandello demonstrate how we choose our own private realities. For Bertolt Brecht the theatre event itself was an occasion for making the audience responsible for restructuring social reality. Implicit in Samuel Beckett's work is a denial of the possibility or even the desirability of meaning in human experience. The reader of modern drama must be ready to play a game in which the rules may change without warning. But even so, modern plays do have some things in common. In this introductory chapter, we survey some of these common characteristics.

The Modern Theatre Event

The development of a new kind of performance environment has enabled and even required modern playwrights to continually change the rules of the dramatic game. Sophocles, Molière, and Shakespeare wrote for actors, audiences, and virtually unchanging playhouses which they knew through intimate daily contact. But the modern dramatist writes for an all-purpose playhouse and a potential world audience.

What is the all-purpose playhouse and how does it affect the modern script? In Part Three we learned that the classical theatre event was based on custom and continuity. The permanent architecture of the playhouse and the traditional expectations of the audience were crucial shaping forces in classical drama. This approach, however, began to change noticeably toward the end of the nineteenth century, with the advent of new concepts intended to revolutionize the nature of dramatic performance.

The first of these was German composer Richard Wagner's vision of the theatre event as a total work of art, or *Gesamtkunstwerk*. In this vision, theatre was no longer defined as unmediated interaction between performer and audience. Instead, the performer was thought of as one element among many, such as music, scenery, costumes, and lighting, which were all under the control of one nonperforming artist—the director. As the total-work-of-art concept grew in influence and directors acquired greater artistic authority, playwrights used more nonacting elements in their plays. Readers of modern drama will notice an increasing reliance on such things as scenery, lights, costumes, music, sound, and props in the modern script. Playwrights now assume that these physical elements can be furnished by any theatre in the world.

The total-work-of-art concept also had consequences for theatre architecture. In 1876, a theatre inspired by Wagner's vision was built in Bayreuth, Germany, in which the old class distinctions of box, pit, and gallery (see chapter 12) were eliminated. All seats were turned to face the stage, and the auditorium lights were darkened during the performance. Rather than observe the responses of the audience along with the play, the spectator was transported, according to Wagner, across a "mystic chasm" into the hypnotic world of dramatic illusion. The *Gesamtkunstwerk* artist thereby extended his control over the audience as well, who were now required to focus their attention on the dramatic space only. Despite various rebellions, the idea of a theatre event dominated by a unified visual field remains a primary force in modern drama.

Ideally, the all-purpose playhouse can do anything the author and the director want it to do. It has no intrusive architectural features of its own and no limiting social or cultural context; it can produce any play. This is, in spirit, the kind of playhouse for which modern scripts are written.

The Modern Script

The typical modern dramatist, then, is a nonconformist spirit who uses the all-purpose playhouse to present a unique view of life as it is to a potentially international audience. Since the time of Ibsen, whose most notorious play, *Ghosts,* premiered in Chicago, Illinois, playwrights have been able to dream of productions from Moscow to Los Angeles and beyond. But performance is not the only medium for the modern playwright's work. Plays appear in book form, also, and gain fame and fortune for their authors through the medium of print.

Ibsen, often referred to as the father of modern drama, can also be considered the father of the modern script. His attention and income were divided equally between publication and performance. His books, as he called his plays, sometimes appeared in print prior to production and were an important medium for the propagation of his art. Writing at a time when mass production and communication were knitting the world into one vast marketplace, Ibsen was the first dramatist to make his voice heard in a sustained body of work for both page and stage.

Another reason for calling Ibsen the inventor of the modern script is his approach to dramatic space. Ibsen began his career as a resident playwright and director in theatres at Bergen and later Christiania (Oslo) in his native Norway. In addition to writing plays for these theatre companies, he was responsible for helping to stage the works of others. He planned the actors' movements, placed the scenery, and designed costumes. When he left Norway to devote himself entirely to writing plays, Ibsen had more than a decade of production experience behind him. This practical background is evident in all his scripts. In committing his plays to print, Ibsen functioned as both director and author, giving the reader not only dialogue but a clear and exact conception of dramatic space. Among the many modern authors who followed in his footsteps, Shaw and O'Neill, especially, regarded print as a vital medium of drama and prepared their scripts accordingly.

Written for the all-purpose playhouse, modern drama is generally conceived in terms of a specific and unique dramatic space. When dramatic space is expressed in production through the movement of actors within a specific physical environment, we call it the *mise en scène*—literally, "what's put on the stage." Since the *mise en scène* is unique for each play, the author must describe it in some detail in his stage directions. These descriptions give the potential director (or *metteur en scène*—"he who puts it on the stage") an indication of the kind of performance the author has envisioned. They are also invaluable to the reader who wants to form a clear picture of the dramatic space and action.

But, while modern stage directions are more explanatory than those of classical scripts, modern dialogue may be less so. This is by no means true of all modern plays. But many authors like to create real images of the surface of daily life by imitating the inconclusive and roundabout way people actually talk. In order to make a good connection with the behavior which underlies this kind of dialogue, the reader must listen closely for clues to the occasions and situations which propel the action. Some modern authors, in fact, achieve their most characteristic effects by putting as little information as possible in the dialogue. Samuel Beckett and Harold Pinter, for instance, are both masters at creating maximum impact with a minimum of dialogue.

Generally speaking, the reader of modern scripts must form an idea of dramatic space solely from the stage directions for a particular play. Modern dramatic space, furthermore, usually represents a reality which is separate from that of the audience. Unlike classical characters, who move easily between the real world of the audience and the fictional world of the play, modern characters tend to stay in their own world. There are, as we might expect, numerous exceptions to this rule. But dramatists who change this rule usually make a point of telling us so in their stage directions. If the dramatic space is meant to include the audience, the author's description of the *mise en scène* will probably tell us exactly how (see, for instance, the excerpts from Peter Shaffer's *Equus* in Script 4).

Conflict

The basic conflict in classical drama, as we have seen, is between the forces of order and chaos in an ideal world. The situation which provokes the action, typically, is a threat of disorder, while the resolution brings the ideal world back into balance—life is once again as it should be. In modern drama, however, the typical conflict is between the ordinary individual and a world that is not ideal. The resolution of this conflict depends on how this individual deals with the recognition of reality. For the modern playwright, this kind of action represents life as it is.

This struggle between the individual and a less than ideal world can be traced in four major conflicts of modern drama. Historically, the first of these has to do with the conflict between women and various social institutions, beginning with marriage. Many theatre historians, in fact, say that modern drama begins with Ibsen's *A Doll's House,* in which the protagonist, Nora Helmer, declares that her first duty is not to the church, the law, or her family, but to herself. At the final curtain she walks out on the first three lesser duties to embrace the remaining great one. The conflict between female self-development and male social ideals is also the subject of *Ghosts* and *Hedda Gabler* and figures prominently in various forms in most of Ibsen's plays.

The battle of the sexes also occurs in the work of Strindberg, who attempted to show, in such plays as *The Father* and *Creditors*, that, far from being the victims of their husbands, women were capable of tormenting and persecuting them to the point of lunacy and death. In *The Dance of Death,* marriage is presented as a kind of living hell that brings out the worst in both male and female.

For Bernard Shaw, woman's struggle against the rigidity and complacency of male institutions became a symbol of the larger struggle of "human vitality vs. artificial system," as critic Eric Bentley describes the Shavian macroconflict. In *Arms and the Man, Candida, Major Barbara, Pygmalion, Heartbreak House, Saint Joan,* and other dramatic works, the reader will discover a steady evolution of the Shavian heroine as she expresses more and more fully what Shaw regards as the most significant aspirations of humanity. His *Man and Superman*, in many respects a traditional comedy of manners, also contains, in a dream sequence, Shaw's philosophy of the "Life Force." While Shaw's male protagonists may talk about the Life Force (and everything else under the sun) his female protagonists embody it. In the typical Shavian recognition, male and female must face some aspect of this truth about one another. The world will never be an ideal place, Shaw seems to imply, until the Life Force can be expressed freely through both men and women.

Bertolt Brecht's characters also struggle perpetually with life as it is in a hostile world. Brecht, however, uses economic and political, rather than male-female, conflicts as his starting point. Among his better-known works are *A Man's A Man, The Threepenny Opera, Saint Joan of the Stockyards, The Private Life of the Master Race, Mother Courage, The Good Woman of Setzuan,* and *The Caucasian Chalk Circle.* As their author did in real life, the characters in these plays struggle against totalitarianism, war, poverty, and displacement. Brecht's method of presenting the dramatic action differs fundamentally from that of his predecessors. While Ibsen and Shaw use the *mise en scène* to create a separate illusion of life as it is, dramatic space in Brecht's scripts includes both explicit and implicit provocation of audience response.

In Russian and American versions of life as it is, the characters pursue dreams of individual happiness without much overt reference to the social context of their behavior. In the plays of Chekhov, O'Neill, Thornton Wilder, Tennessee Williams, and Sam Shepard, the obstacle to this happiness lies in the incompatibility of dreams and reality rather than in the hostility of specific social institutions. Chekhov's characters fail to realize their dreams because they prefer dreaming to grappling with reality. O'Neill's characters destroy themselves in the pursuit of pipe dreams. In Wilder's *Our Town,* Emily Webb returns from the grave only to discover that the living do not truly realize they are alive. Williams' characters are fatally attracted to what Tom, in *The Glass*

Menagerie, calls "that long delayed but always expected something we live for." In Shepard's work, the inner dream and outer reality merge into a permanent hallucination in which the individual finds it impossible to identify what really stands in the way. Social issues are more in evidence in the plays of Arthur Miller, Lorraine Hansberry, and Imamu Amiri Baraka, although less clearly in the foreground than in the plays of Ibsen, Shaw, and Brecht.

In addition to the pursuits of justice, individual happiness, and wholeness through male-female struggle, another conflict in modern drama involves the pursuit of visionary truth. In the works of Strindberg, Pirandello, Beckett, and others, an effort is made to penetrate the surface of everyday life as it is, seen from the outside, and reveal to the audience a more timeless vision of life as it is, seen from a more eternal, and internal, perspective. The protagonists of Strindberg's *A Dream Play* and *The Ghost Sonata* explore the symbolic world of dreams in an effort to understand and reconcile themselves to human suffering. The characters in Pirandello's *Right You Are, If You Think You Are* and *Six Characters in Search of an Author* test the assumption that there is such a thing as objective reality. In the moment of recognition, this truth is faced: distinctions between illusion and reality are purely personal. In Beckett's *Waiting for Godot* and *Endgame,* four characters face an empty and indifferent universe expecting nothing, but nevertheless expecting.

As *we* might expect, these many-sided conflicts of modern drama are rarely expressed through the traditional structures of classical comedy and tragedy. Instead, modern dramatists have invented a variety of new structures in which comic and tragic elements coexist and merge with one another. When *The Cherry Orchard* was first produced at the Moscow Art Theatre in 1904, author Chekhov and director Stanislavski were in total disagreement over what kind of play it was. Chekhov said it was a comedy; Stanislavski said it was a tragedy. Although the dispute was never resolved, the production was a great success. Apparently the play was both or neither. In any case, the traditional concepts of tragedy and comedy proved to be irrelevant (although Chekhov had the last word, calling it a comedy in the published script). Today we would be more likely to call *The Cherry Orchard* a realistic drama than a comedy or a tragedy. It is realism, in fact, which provides the starting point for most of the diverse structures of modern drama.

But what is realism? A dramatic representation of reality, evidently. Then what is reality? Do Ibsen's plays contain the same reality as O'Neill's, or Chekhov's, or Shaw's? Clearly not. What these authors have in common, however, is an effort to present life as it is by showing us the familiar surface of our everyday behavior. Each realist selects different aspects of this behavior, and each creates different structures to dramatize those realities he finds most compelling.

And, as has been suggested above, not all playwrights agree that recognizable daily behavior is what drama should be about. To many modern dramatists, including some who began their careers as realists, the fascination and excitement of life and drama are to be found in the exploration of extraordinary and unfamiliar states of being. Playwrights thus inspired have created works which dramatize the subjective realm of dreams, or penetrating metaphysical speculation, or the disappearance of meaning and purpose. A wide variety of critical terms—expressionism, theatricalism, Pirandellism, epic realism, absurdism—have been invented to label modern plays which are reactions against realism and yet are not attempts to revive the conventions of classical drama. For the sake of convenience we will call such plays antirealistic.

Contradiction

A final characteristic of modern drama which the reader can expect to encounter is its frequent appeal to contradictory responses. This appeal is by no means absent from classical drama. In chapter 10, for instance, we noticed how Sophocles presents Oedipus' character in ironic perspective—we empathize with his need to save the city, yet we know that he is wrong to blame Teiresias and Creon for his troubles. But the spirit of contradiction, or irony, works in a different way in modern drama, in which comedy and tragedy merge, and every strong force seems to inspire its opposite.

Ibsen, for instance, was intensely ironic in temperament. He liked to meditate on such quixotic ideas as a fish afraid of water or an owl afraid of the dark. "There must be troll in what I write," he once stated, meaning that he wished to give the mischievous side of his nature equal play with his earnestness. Ibsen's sympathetic characters often behave meanly, and his righteous characters can be cold and selfish. Poised on a razor's edge of contrary responses to life, Ibsen's plays contain great comic potential. Alert readers will catch glimpses of a gleeful imp hidden in the folds of the melodramatic fabric in which the plays are often dressed by producers and critics.

Strindberg was particularly sensitive to the painful side of comic situations. "It is not witty but idiotic," he wrote, "to laugh at what a man in his daily life takes seriously, perhaps tragically." In *The Father,* the hero feels that his situation is tragic. His wife finds him ridiculous. Ridiculous because he is tragic and tragic because he is ridiculous, he finally loses his sanity. Another of Strindberg's characters says, "I feel like a circus child being pinched behind the scenes, to look rosy to the crowd." Strindberg asks us to think, feel, weep, and laugh all at the same time. This fusion of contrary responses gives his plays a feeling of sustained discord.

"I hate to see people comfortable," Shaw wrote, "when they ought to be uncomfortable." He enjoyed turning familiar dramatic conventions on their heads to demonstrate that the old idealistic theatre and the public were ridiculous for believing in them. In *Man and Superman,* Jack Tanner and Ann Whitefield finally declare their love for one another, and Jack announces their engagement to the assembled company. "I solemnly declare," he says at this happy-ending moment, "that I am not a happy man." He goes on to say that marriage is the end of happiness and the beginning of service to the Life Force.

At his side a smug Ann Whitefield advises him to "just keep on talking" as the curtain falls to "universal laughter."

Pirandello was also fascinated by the possibility of contrary responses. In his essay "Humor" he uses the example of an old woman who makes herself ridiculous by wearing the clothes and makeup of a young girl. The contradiction between her age and appearance provoke a "knowledge of the contrary," which inspires laughter. When we learn, however, that she is destitute and can only keep the attention of her lover by dressing as she does, a "feeling of the contrary" arises and we pity her. In his plays Pirandello created a world of contrary perceptions and obsessively asked, Which is reality? In *Six Characters in Search of an Author,* a whole family appears in a theatre in search of a point of view which will make them real. Pirandello's answer to the reality question is summed up in the title of another of his plays, *Right You Are, If You Think You Are.*

O'Neill's characters struggle to distinguish love from hate. Whenever they assert one feeling, they are ambushed by its opposite. At the end of Act II of *Long Day's Journey Into Night,* Mary Tyrone talks to herself after saying goodbye to her husband and sons:

> MARY: It's so lonely here. [*Then her face hardens into bitter self-contempt.*] You're lying to yourself again. You wanted to get rid of them. Their contempt and disgust aren't pleasant company. You're glad they're gone. [*She gives a despairing little laugh.*] Then Mother of God, why do I feel so lonely?

It is said that Ibsen, bedridden at seventy-eight, contradicted his nurse one day when she said he was looking better. "On the contrary," he said. The next day he died without further comment. These famous last words were appropriate for the father of modern drama. Contradiction is what the reader of modern scripts can count on. Images of reality—the playwright's personal vision of life as it is—abound. But whose reality is real? Illusions of reality and the reality of the theatre event declare war. Audiences look at themselves in the fun-house mirrors of modern drama and don't know whether to laugh or cry. Like Dionysus, the Greek god of the theatre, the modern gods of drama die a thousand deaths, are fragmented and dispersed, and then are miraculously reborn in surprising shapes and unexpected places. The reader of modern drama must be prepared for anything and everything.

14 ❧ *The* Mise en Scène

*I*f we look at the theatre event in broad historical perspective, we can distinguish four major phases. Greek tragedy was performed against the background of the cosmos, defined as the earth below, the sky above, and the gods watching over all. Shakespeare's theatre was partly enclosed and partly open, seeming to embrace both the natural world of the ancients and the artificial world of the future. In neoclassical times, drama became completely divorced from nature as performances moved indoors. In the modern script, the influence of the playhouse itself tends to recede, as another artificial environment—the *mise en scène*—becomes the prime shaper of dramatic space.*

Each of the first three phases was dominated by one kind of playhouse. In the modern era, there is every kind of playhouse, including replicas of the classical amphitheatre. Although, historically speaking, certain kinds of stage are closely associated with certain authors (the proscenium stage with the early realists, for instance), contemporary theatre practice operates on the assumption that most scripts will work on most stages, if there is sufficient creativity—and technology—available to fulfill at least the spirit of the author's *mise en scène*. For the reader of modern scripts, the *mise en scène* is much more relevant than the playhouse in imagining dramatic action.

Before turning to a brief survey of the development of the modern *mise en scène*, we should review the meanings of three related terms: dramatic space, setting, and *mise en scène*. Dramatic space is that combination of setting and simultaneous behavior we create in our imaginations while reading the script. Setting tells us where the characters are. While classical scripts give only a general indication of setting, modern scripts usually describe a specific setting which is unique for each play. The *mise en scène,* as we use the term, consists of the specifications not only for setting and movement, but for lighting, costumes, props (moveable objects handled by the characters), and sound as we imagine them functioning in the dramatic action. (The term *mise en scène* is also used, by directors and designers, to refer to the physical aspects of a setting of a particular production. This concept of the *mise en scène* may sometimes come into conflict with the author's script).

---

*Some observers may even wish to distinguish another phase, in which the three-dimensional *mise en scène* is replaced by electronically generated images of action projected directly onto the retina by means of a cathode-ray tube. Called television, or video, this phase of drama, however, no longer qualifies as a theatre event, nor are its scripts usually available, or interesting, to the general reader.

123

❧ *Playwright and Director Clash Over Mise en Scène*

The following story by Samuel G. Freedman appeared in *The New York Times* on December 13, 1984, under the headline " 'Endgame' Opens in Wake of Pact":

Lawyers for Samuel Beckett and the American Repertory Theatre reached an out-of-court settlement late yesterday allowing the theater's revival of "Endgame" to proceed. The opening-night curtain rose on the production only hours after the agreement was signed.

The settlement averted a court battle about the production's departures from Mr. Beckett's stage directions. Until the agreement was reached, lawyers for both sides had been preparing briefs and contacting potential witnesses.

In the settlement, the theater agreed to include in all "Endgame" programs the first page of the published play—which includes Mr. Beckett's description of the set—and statements from Mr. Beckett and Grove Press, his American publisher, denouncing the production as "completely unacceptable" and "a complete parody of the play as conceived by me." The theater also agreed to use those statements in any advertisements or promotions for "Endgame" that use Mr. Beckett's name.

Tried to Stop Production
Grove Press and Mr. Beckett made concessions in return. They allowed the revival to proceed rather than fight it in court. And they permitted the theater to insert in the program and any advertisements a statement defending the integrity and fidelity of its production of "Endgame."

The dispute began last week when Barney Rosset—Mr. Beckett's American theatrical agent and the president of Grove Press—demanded that the American Repertory Theater halt the production. He contended that the theatre was distorting the play by setting it in an underground subway station, rather than the bare, cell-like room the playwright had specified in his stage directions.

Martin Garbus, an attorney for the playwright and Grove Press, said yesterday that he decided to settle out of court for several reasons. A court case, he said, would have proved expensive and would have lasted several weeks, even as "Endgame" gave performances. He added that unless Mr. Beckett appeared as a witness—which he said the playwright did not want to do—he was not certain he could win an injunction against the production. But he added that he felt the out-of-court settlement would dissuade other theaters from veering from Mr. Beckett's text and stage directions.

Ibsen's Living Room

From *A Doll's House* in 1879 to Sam Shepard's *Buried Child,* which won the Pulitzer Prize in 1979, the family living room—or drawing room or parlor—is arguably the predominant *mise en scène* in modern drama. Other domestic interiors, especially kitchens and bedrooms, run a close second. In some plays several rooms are used, and often the house's exterior is also included, as in O'Neill's *Desire Under the Elms* and *Death of a Salesman.* For the modern playwright, life as it is usually begins at home.

Ibsen established the domestic *mise en scène* as the home base of modern dramatic space in that cycle of eleven plays, written over a period of twenty years, which includes *A Doll's House, Ghosts, Rosmersholm,* and *Hedda Gabler.* Only in his final work, *When We Dead Awaken,* did Ibsen return completely to the mountainside settings of his early romantic phase. But, although there are many domestic settings in Ibsen, each is a unique expression of the particular drama for which it was created. In a proscenium theatre, the kind Ibsen learned in and wrote for, the *mise en scène* is seen by the audience through a large opening, called the proscenium arch, in the wall (proscenium) which separates the stage from the audience. This is sometimes called the fourth wall method of staging since, when the curtain which covers the opening rises or parts, the audience sees, typically, three walls; the fourth, situated between the audience and the stage, is assumed to be invisible. (The term *box set* is also used to describe a *mise en scène* which presents the audience with a fourth wall view of three walls and possibly a ceiling.)

Since Ibsen prepared his scripts as both author and director, we should pay careful attention to his descriptions of the *mise en scène.* The details of the setting and the indications of simultaneous behavior are important to an understanding of the dramatic action. Script 14 contains stage directions from his 1891 drama, *Hedda Gabler.* The setting contains many elements which figure importantly in the action; the french windows, the tile stove, and the grand piano all have special roles to play. The inner room, with the general's portrait above the sofa, is of particular interest. As the action unfolds, we learn that the general is Hedda's father, now dead. Whenever the curtain is open to the inner room, we can see the general looking down on the characters. Notice, in Act II, how Ibsen places Tesman, Hedda's husband, and Brack, her admirer, in the inner room, under the portrait. When Hedda sits on the living room sofa with Lövborg, her former lover, on her left, they have their backs to the inner room. Tesman and Brack can observe what they *appear* to be doing—looking at a photo album. But the audience will see what they are *really* doing— whispering about their meetings in younger days, when the general watched over them in life, as he now appears to do in death. In Act IV, Tesman flings back the curtain on the inner room and discovers that Hedda has shot herself. Once again, the portrait of the dead general dominates the dramatic space.

Ibsen's plays are carefully crafted and his scripts embody this craft. For this reason and many others, Ibsen's drama provides a rich storehouse of

Script 14
From Henrik Ibsen's
Hedda Gabler (English version by Kari Borg).

Act I. [*A spacious and attractive living room, decorated in dark colors. In the rear wall a wide opening, with curtains pulled aside, revealing an inner room, in the same style as the living room. In the right wall of the living room is a double door leading to the hall. In the left wall are french windows with open curtains. Through the windows we see a veranda and autumn foliage. Downstage is an oval table covered with a cloth and surrounded by chairs. Down right, a large, dark porcelain stove, a high-backed armchair, a footstool, and two hassocks. In the corner up right, a sofa and small round table. Above the french windows is a grand piano. On either side of the rear opening are shelves containing ornaments. In the inner room, we see a sofa, a table, and several chairs. On the wall above the sofa is an oil portrait of a handsome, elderly man in a general's uniform. . . .*]

reading experience. His plays also provide an excellent introduction to that continuing tradition in modern drama which transforms a familiar domestic environment into highly charged dramatic space.

The Room Disappears

By using the fourth wall method, the playwright can tell secrets while pretending not to. The family living room, whether it is Hedda Gabler's or Mama Younger's, is a private place. Looking through the fourth wall, we have a Peeping Tom's view of the intimate life of the family. This view of dramatic space is highly suited to one of the major themes of modern drama—the revelation of private behavior.

But, although it has been in steady use for more than a century, the realistic domestic interior is by no means the only type of setting to be found in the modern script. August Strindberg, Ibsen's contemporary, sought to extend the audience's view of intimate behavior by exposing the innermost workings of his own psyche. To do this, he invented new kinds of *mise en scène*.

While Ibsen worked methodically and steadily, publishing another version of his living room every two years, Strindberg brought to the drama a more experimental temperament. The living room of his play *The Father* has an unusual, but not unrealistic, feature—a door papered like the surrounding wall. The hero of the play is at one point locked up behind the door but bursts

Act II. [TESMAN *and* BRACK *move into the inner rooms and sit down. During the following conversation they can be seen drinking brandy, smoking, and talking. . . .* HEDDA *sits in the sofa in the living room, placing a photo album on the table in front of her.* LOVBORG *moves closer and watches her. Then he takes a chair and sits at her left, his back toward the inner room. . . .* BRACK *stays in the inner room, keeping an occasional eye on* LÖVBORG *and* HEDDA.]

Act IV. [HEDDA *goes into the inner room, closing the curtains. After a brief pause, we hear her playing a wild dance on the piano. . . . A shot is heard from the inner room.* TESMAN, MRS. ELVSTED, *and* BRACK *rise. . . .* TESMAN, *followed by* MRS. ELVSTED, *rushes to open the curtains.* HEDDA *lies on the sofa, lifeless.*]

In stage directions for modern plays, the words *down, up, left* and *right* often appear. Left and right are from the actor's point of view. If we remember that stages used to be raked, or tilted, with their lower edge toward the audience, we will realize that up means away from the audience and down towards it. Similarly with *above* and *below*.

through it when his madness begins to overwhelm him, as if thrusting himself through the wall itself. This effect of penetrating walls was carried even further by Strindberg in subsequent plays.

Strindberg's scripts, like Ibsen's, lay out the *mise en scène* in great detail. Script 15 contains about one-third of the stage directions which describe the settings of the three scenes of his 1907 drama, *The Ghost Sonata*. In the first scene, we are told, the curtains on the Round Room windows will be opened during the action, giving us a partial view of the interior of the room, which contains a statue. In scene 2 we are taken into the Round Room and given a closer view of the statue as well as the rest of the room. A door in the Round Room now provides a view of the Hyacinth Room, the setting for scene 3. Strindberg's settings, taken in sequence, create a feeling of movement— through the window into the Round Room, through the door into the Hyacinth Room—from one to another. This movement parallels an important aspect of the dramatic action—the penetration of the facade of everyday life. In the stage direction which climaxes this exploration of dramatic space, "the room disappears" and is replaced by the image of a painting, Arnold Böcklin's *The Isle of the Dead.* The theme of penetrating the mystery of life is carried to its final conclusion in this painting, which shows a boat entering the harbor of the island where mortals go after death. Other aspects of the *mise en scène*— the window mirror in which the street goings-on can be seen from the house, a cupboard containing a mummy, and a death screen, used to shield the dying from view—provide an appropriate environment for the characters in *The*

Script 15
From August Strindberg's
The Ghost Sonata (English version by Kari Borg).

Scene 1. [*The facade of a house on a city street. At the corner of the ground floor is the Round Room. A balcony with a flagpole at the corner of the second floor. The windows of the Round Room face both the main street and a side street. When the scene begins the curtains on these windows are closed. When they are opened, later in the action, we see, in the sunlight, a white marble statue of a young woman, surrounded by palms.*]

Scene 2. [*Interior of the Round Room. Upstage is a white porcelain stove, a mirror, and a candelabra. To the right of the stove is a hallway entrance, providing a partial view of the Green Room, with mahogany furniture. On the left is a closet door, papered like the wall. An open curtain reveals the statue, shaded by palms. Upstage left is the door to the Hyacinth Room, where the* YOUNG LADY *is seen reading. In the Green Room, we see the* COLONEL'S *back as he sits writing.*]

Scene 3. [*Interior of the Hyacinth Room. . . . The room disappears. Böcklin's picture* The Isle of the Dead *appears in the distance. Music— soft, sweet, melancholy—comes from the island.*]

Ghost Sonata, whose behavior seems to take place on both the natural and the supernatural planes. The *mise en scène* is conceived with equal care in Strindberg's many other antirealistic works.

The Electric Stage

How can a room disappear and be replaced by a painting? Can such a fluid idea of dramatic space be realized in a practical *mise en scène?* The answer is yes—if we apply modern technology. In 1879, the year of *A Doll's House,* Thomas Edison invented the electric light. Strindberg was well aware of this new potential. For a production of *A Dream Play,* he urged the producer to use a new electric device, the stereopticon, to project the flow of scenic images the play requires. An author of great vision, his conception of dramatic space was in tune with the future. It was not long before electricity found its way into the theatre and flexible lighting became the hallmark of the modern *mise en scène,* controlling the scope, texture, and mood of everything the audience saw. Before long, playwrights were routinely including indications of lighting in their stage directions. Modern dramatic space came to be shaped by electric light in its very conception.

Script 16
From Arthur Miller's
Death of a Salesman.

A

[*The entire setting is wholly or, in some places, partially transparent. The roof-line of the house is one-dimensional; under and over it we see the apartment buildings. Before the house lies an apron, curving beyond the forestage into the orchestra. This forward area serves as the back yard as well as the locale of all Willy's imaginings and of his city scenes. Whenever the action is in the present, the actors observe the imaginary wall-lines, entering the house only through its door at the left. But in the scenes of the past these boundaries are broken, and characters enter or leave a room by stepping "through" a wall onto the forestage.*]

[WILLY'S *form is dimly seen below in the darkened kitchen. He opens the refrigerator, searches in there, and takes out a bottle of milk. The apartment houses are fading out, and the entire house and surroundings become covered with leaves.*]

B

[UNCLE BEN, *carrying a valise and an umbrella, enters the forestage around the right corner of the house. . . . He enters exactly as* WILLY *speaks.*]
WILLY: I'm getting awfully tired, Ben.
[BEN'S *music is heard.* BEN *looks around at everything.*]
CHARLEY: Good, keep playing; you'll sleep better. Did you call me Ben?
[BEN *looks at his watch.*]
WILLY: That's funny. For a second there you reminded me of my brother Ben.
BEN: I only have a few minutes. [*He strolls, inspecting the place.* WILLY *and* CHARLEY *continue playing.*]

C

[*Music is heard as behind a scrim, to the left of the house.* THE WOMAN, *dimly seen, is dressing.*]

D

[*. . . All move toward the audience, through the wall-line of the kitchen. At the limit of the apron,* LINDA *lays down the flowers, kneels, and sits back on her heels. All stare down at the grave.*]

By the time Arthur Miller's *Death of a Salesman* was first performed in 1949, making a room disappear was well within the capacity of theatre technology. Miller's working title for this play was "The Inside of His Head." Script 16 contains excerpts from this play which show how the *mise en scène* embodies this inside out point of view, as well as an objective realism.

In excerpt A we learn that the setting is "partially transparent" with "imaginary wall-lines" and houses which "fade out" or "become covered with leaves." In B, Willy plays cards with his neighbor, Charley, as he talks to his brother, Ben, in his imagination. Ben is seen by the audience but not by Charley. In C a "scrim"—fabric which can hide or reveal according to how it is lit—gives momentary physical presence to an image in Willy's memory. In D, the "apron," or the edge of the stage nearest the audience, represents Willy's final resting place. This area is also used as a restaurant, Willy's back yard, and other settings, past and present. Always in the background is the interior of Willy's house—a kitchen and two bedrooms. They appear and disappear through the use of light. This fluid dramatic space expresses both objective reality—life as it is, seen from the outside—and the mixture of fantasy and memory which is the inside of Willy's head.

The Audience Makes a Comeback

This half-century of development of the *mise en scène* took place mainly within the picture frame of the proscenium arch. For the most part, the audience was left out. When they were included, it was a novelty. In *Strange Interlude* O'Neill reinvented the aside to help his characters reveal their feelings directly. In Wilder's *Our Town,* the Stage Manager regularly addresses the public, as does Tom in Williams' *The Glass Menagerie.* Even so, the architectural rigidity of the proscenium theatre worked in favor of actor-audience separation, as did electric light. Not only does modern theatrical lighting intensify the actor's presence and de-emphasize the audience, but blinding spotlights also hide the audience from the onstage actor.

Parallel with the growing importance of theatrical lighting was the development of modern cinema. Early movies, projecting drama onto a screen the shape of a proscenium picture frame, looked like photographed plays. These photoplays, however, could be mass-produced and distributed in a way that the custom-made products of the live theatre could not. As movies established profitability, they also developed their unique artistry. The camera, it was discovered, could move, creating an infinite possibility of visual fields. Space could be cut into pieces and reassembled in any way desired. In close-ups, flashbacks, and montage editing, movies taught the audience a new way of looking at drama.

By mid-century, the theatre and the movies looked very much alike. Both had a lighted frame in one end of the space and an audience in the dark in the other. But the technological challenge of the movies soon provoked growing awareness among theatre artists that live drama could be more than just a creative *mise en scène*. The theatre event itself was full of possibilities for experimentation.

This experimentation took place—and continues to take place—in all aspects of live drama: in writing, acting, directing, design, and theatre architecture. Although countless artists have contributed to the development of the modern theatre event, one name stands out among the others—that of German poet, playwright, director, and theorist, Bertolt Brecht. Realists such as Ibsen, Shaw, Chekhov, Arthur Miller, and Lorraine Hansberry use the *mise en scène* to create illusions of life as it is in the presence of an "invisible" audience. Brecht, on the other hand, calls attention to the artificiality of the *mise en scène*, and the reality of the theatre event—especially its social nature. Live drama, he felt, ought to show the audience how to take responsibility for the society whose values the theatre is meant to express.

Experiments in connecting the dramatic space with the audience are ongoing in the modern theatre. Characters in plays set in more or less realistic living rooms now communicate freely with the audience. In Peter Nichols' *A Day in the Death of Joe Egg* and John Guare's *The House of Blue Leaves*, for instance, characters not only talk to the audience but entertain us with music and song. Even Neil Simon, a habitual fourth waller, has Eugene, the young hero of *Brighton Beach Memoirs,* talking to the audience against the realistic background of the family home. In *The Mystery of Edwin Drood*, the English music hall setting includes the theatre itself, as actors stop the performance of an unfinished story by Charles Dickens to ask the real audience to vote on the ending. And the proscenium stage continues to function. Such avant-garde authors as Samuel Beckett and Sam Shepard, pursuing a more radically subjective dramatic image than Ibsen, nevertheless, continue to explore the potential of dramatic space seen through an invisible fourth wall.

To sum up, the modern script, viewed historically, shows an increasing reliance on a *mise en scène* which is created technologically, primarily through the use of lighting and reflects narrative techniques drawn from cinema. Because both the technological *mise en scène* and the fourth wall point of view tend to separate audience and actor, modern drama is also characterized by a variety of efforts to maintain actor-audience interaction. Any or all of these historical developments may be reflected in the stage directions of the modern script.

Poetry of the Theatre

As modern theatre artists became increasingly aware of the dramatic potential of the nondialogue theatrical elements of scenery, lights, costumes, music, sound, props, and movement, the *mise en scène* began to take on a life of its own. French director Jacques Copeau gave a name to this new dramatic force—poetry of the theatre. This effect is certainly present in the examples we have already looked at, in which essential aspects of dramatic action are expressed through the *mise en scène*. A few further examples, however, will help bring this special intensification of the *mise en scène* more sharply into focus.

Anton Chekhov's *The Cherry Orchard* tells the story of the loss of a family estate. In the first act the mother, Lyubov Andreyevna, returns home after a long absence. Her homecoming takes place in the nursery, where her life, and her daughter's, began. She weeps with joy when she sees the room, still unchanged since her childhood.

> LYUBOV: I used to sleep in this nursery. I used to look at the orchard from this window. I woke up happy every morning, and here it all is, the same as ever . . .

Her daughter, Anya, echoes her sentiments as she goes about the room touching the furniture and looking out the window at the cherry trees in bloom. Acts II and III take place in other settings, but the last act curtain rises again on the nursery. The occasion this time, however, is not homecoming but leave-taking. The house and grounds have been sold, and the family is splitting up. The room is completely changed in appearance and feeling:

> Act IV: [*Same setting as Act I. There are no curtains on the windows or pictures on the walls. The room is bare except for a few pieces of furniture, arranged in a corner as if for sale. Suitcases and bundles stand near the door.*]

At last everyone leaves and the nursery is empty. The play is about to end.

> [*In the silence we hear the sound of an axe striking a tree. Then footsteps.* FIRS *enters the room. He is very ill.*]

Firs, the eighty-seven-year-old servant, has been left behind in the confusion. The main door of the room has been locked from the outside. Realizing what has happened and too weak to do anything about it, Firs lies down on the floor. This is the final visual image of the play—the dying servant abandoned in the empty nursery. Memories of the joyous homecoming of the first act contrast vividly with the cold emptiness of the last.

Although the empty nursery provides the final visual image, sound, too, plays an important role. As Firs loses consciousness, we hear the axe cutting into the cherry trees, destroying this symbol of a whole way of life. And along with this sound there is one other, "a sad, dying sound, as if the string of a violin is breaking." This sound has been heard before, in the second act, when the family was gathered in a field on the estate, enjoying the out-of-doors. When the sound is heard, no one can identify it.

> LYUBOV: What's that?
> LOPAHIN: I don't know. Maybe a cable has snapped and a bucket fallen down a mine. But far off in the distance.
> GAEV: Could it be a bird? Maybe a heron?

TROFIMOV: Or an owl.

LYUBOV [*shuddering*]: Unpleasant, for some reason. [*Pause.*]

FIRS: It was like this before the disaster. The owls hooted and the samovar hummed and no one knew why.

GAEV: Before what disaster?

FIRS: Before the serfs were set free.

When the sound is heard for the second time, ending the play, we do not know if Firs hears it or not. But the audience hears it, and we are left to make our own interpretation. Is it the sound of disaster? Of the family—and Firs— being set free? Or both? This mysterious sound provides, in all its ambiguity, the resolution of *The Cherry Orchard*.

The plays of American dramatist Tennessee Williams also contain much that could be called poetry of the theatre. In *The Glass Menagerie*, Williams gives the reader an evocative description of the lighting in the "Production Notes" which introduce the script:

> The lighting in the play is not realistic. In keeping with the atmosphere of memory, the stage is dim. Shafts of light are focused on selected areas of actors, sometimes in contradistinction to what is the apparent center. . . . A certain correspondence to light in religious paintings, such as El Greco's, where the figures are radiant in atmosphere that is relatively dusky, could be effectively used throughout the play.

In addition to lighting, Williams calls for several kinds of music. Laura comforts herself by playing "old, worn-out records" on her phonographs. These phonographs belonged to her father, who has abandoned the family. In addition, music drifts into the family apartment from the Paradise Dance Hall across the alley. This music is heard when Jim, the boy Laura loved in high school, invites her to dance. Williams also calls for incidental music "to give emotional emphasis to suitable passages." This music is identified with Laura and her collection of glass animals:

> When you look at a piece of delicately spun glass you think of two things: how beautiful it is and how easily it can be broken. Both of these ideas should be woven into the recurring tune . . .

Not only the stage directions but the action of the play, and all Williams' plays, stimulate the mind's musical ear.

Laura's collection of "scores of transparent glass animals" are the most important props. "The lovely fragility of the glass," Williams tells us, "is her image." This glass menagerie, always visible in the living room setting, is directly involved in the action at two important moments. At the end of scene 3, Tom flings off his coat in anger and accidentally shatters some of the animals. Laura is nearly destroyed, and Tom is devastated with shame. This physical "business" dramatizes the essence of Tom's relationship to Laura. He is trapped and violently angry but cannot bear to hurt her by bursting out of

❧ *Prop Upstages Actor*

In his autobiography, *Early Stages,* John Gielgud recalls his performance in the role of Konstantin Treplev in Chekhov's *The Sea Gull:*

> Konstantin is a very romantic character, a sort of miniature Hamlet, and a very exciting part for a young actor. I was given very good notices on the whole, and thought at first that I was very well suited to the part. I resented the laughter of the audience when I came on in the second act holding a dead seagull, but on a very small stage it did look rather like a stuffed Christmas goose, however carefully I arranged its wings and legs beforehand.

his trap. In scene 7 another clumsy male, Jim, the gentleman caller, knocks a glass unicorn off a table, breaking its horn. This time Laura doesn't seem nearly as hurt, which tells us much about her state of mind when she is alone with Jim.

Three Ways to Read a Play

Modern drama presents the reader with images of action in an individualized *mise en scène.* These may be images of familiar, everyday behavior, or they may represent the subjective world inside someone's head; very often they are a combination of both. Sometimes the action includes the audience and sometimes we are asked to view it through an invisible fourth wall. The nature of the images and the role of the audience depend, not on a single tradition of dramatic modernism, but on the way each author envisions the *mise en scène* for each particular play.

An understanding of the *mise en scène* is a crucial step in the process of imagining dramatic action. But it need not be the first step. Some readers may wish, in their first reading of a script, to plunge directy into the action by concentrating on empathic connection with the characters' behavior, and, in a second reading, focus on how the scenery, lighting, costumes, props, and sound condition the behavior. Other readers may want to begin by finding out as much as they can about the *mise en scène,* and bring their powers of empathy to bear on the characters in the second reading. In either case the two elements, *mise en scène* and behavior, can be synthesized into a total dramatic experience in a third reading. It doesn't matter which step comes first. What matters is that all steps be taken. A play, like a poem, is a highly condensed form of literature. The riches of drama must be earned by a careful and creative mining of the script.

15 ❧ Realism

> *The trouble with literary terms is that in proportion as they become impressive they become useless, in proportion as they become exact they become inapplicable. A literary term changes color while you watch it; the only rule must be to watch it carefully. It must not be imagined, for example, that the word realism could ever be a summary of a good writer's work. The term will not include one hundred per cent of his art, nor will his art include one hundred per cent of the meanings of realism.*
>
> —Eric Bentley
> Drama Critic

*R*ealism is a means, not an end, a starting point, not a goal, in modern drama. The realist shows us characters who are ordinary people, usually in a familiar domestic setting, usually seen through an invisible fourth wall by a hidden audience. But the realist uses these illusions of momentary existence to show us, in the end, something that is deeply true about human life. Ibsen and Williams transform ordinary objects and incidents into symbolic statements about human destiny. Shaw uses brilliant wit and explosive rhetoric to articulate fully his characters' personal, social, economic, and political positions. Strindberg, in his early realistic plays, demonstrates the operation of hidden forces—for example, the power of suggestion—in daily life. O'Neill's tormented characters are conceived with such intensity that they seem to embody an eternal human condition.

One of the ways the reader of drama can find his way through the varieties of modern realism is to identify the major conflict of the work at hand. In this chapter we discuss four important macroconflicts found in modern drama: male vs. female; the individual vs. social injustice; human consciousness vs. the mystery of life; and the personal dream vs. the real world. Individual variations and combinations are numerous, as we might expect, and few plays can be reduced to a single formulation. But, used with imagination and empathy, these conflicts can provide a beginning framework for an eventually more subtle and complex reading experience.

Another important aspect of modern realism is the author's approach to plot. In the final section of this chapter we examine some of the differences between linear and mosaic realism.

Male vs. Female

Ibsen, Strindberg, and Shaw, three outstanding playwrights, developed the male-female conflict extensively in a number of realistic plays. The issue was not an end in itself, and it eventually led each author down a different path. But the reader of such plays as *A Doll's House, Ghosts, Hedda Gabler, The Father, Miss Julie, Arms and the Man, Man and Superman,* or *Pygmalion*—to mention a few prominent titles—will find that this conflict generates a great deal of the dramatic action.

Ibsen's three protagonists pursue a similar objective—to fulfill and express their individuality and humanity. Nora, in *A Doll's House,* wants her husband, Torvald, to recognize her for what she truly is, a devoted wife and a competent human being. In *Ghosts,* Mrs. Alving wants to be free of the tainted reputation and money of her dead husband and to love her son, Oswald, without guilt or regret. Hedda Gabler wants to live underground and to see her desires and ambitions realized through the men in her life. The obstacle which faces each of the women is the same: the male power structure. In Ibsen, social power is in the hands of the male professional class. Bankers, doctors, pastors, judges, and military men keep strict control over the life of the community and the behavior of subordinates and women. Expressions of individuality on the part of the powerless are treated as frivolity or a sign of moral degeneracy. When Nora recognizes that her banker husband is incapable of recognizing *her* as a separate human being, she walks out on him. Mrs. Alving, in *Ghosts,* once tried to leave her negligent husband, only to be sent back to her wifely duties by the man she secretly loved, Pastor Manders. In the course of the play she undergoes a series of harrowing recognitions as various ghosts of the past return. These recognitions climax in the final moments of play when Oswald, apparently suffering from congenital syphilis of the brain, begins to lose his sanity and begs to be put to death. Hedda Gabler finally recognizes that her husband, Professor Tesman, and her admirer, Judge Brack, are both unaware of and indifferent to her real desires in life and chooses suicide as the only form of self-expression open to her.

Strindberg's male-female power struggles are presented in the context of social class as well as marital conflict. Strindberg was fascinated by what he called soul murder, the process whereby one character probes an area of emotional weakness in another through the power of suggestion. The protagonist of *The Father,* called the Captain, is driven mad by his wife, Laura, when she suggests to him that he may not be the father of their child. When the Captain recognizes that his suspicion will never be confirmed—Laura cleverly refuses to offer proof—he ends up in a straitjacket. Her brother, a pastor, sees what has happened:

PASTOR: Look in the mirror! You don't dare!

LAURA: I never look in the mirror.

PASTOR: No, you don't dare face yourself. Let me see your hand. Not one tell-tale bloodstain, not a trace of poison, . . . crime the law can't touch, a crime you're hardly aware of. A stroke of genius!

The protagonist of *Miss Julie* is a young countess who seeks excitement with her father's ambitious and cynical valet, Jean. Sensing that she wishes to degrade herself, Jean first seduces, then insults her. When she recognizes the power he has gained over her, she is seized with terror and her will crumbles. "Give me an order," she says, "and I'll obey like a dog." Jean hands her a razor and whispers in her ear. Julie thanks him and walks through the door on her way to the barn, as the curtain falls. In later "soul murder" plays, men destroy men (*Creditors*) and women destroy women (*The Stronger*). But the roots of these actions lie in Strindberg's perception of the male-female conflict.

For Shaw, male-female conflict was a potential source of human creativity. In *Arms and the Man*, Raina achieves her objective of living a more real life by choosing a man who sees through her fakery. Jack Tanner, protagonist of *Man and Superman*, discovers that all the philosophy in the world will not save him from marrying Ann Whitefield, once she has made up her mind. "The Life Force," he cries when he recognizes what is happening to him, "I am in the grip of the Life Force." Ann does not understand what Jack means. "It sounds like the Life Guards," she replies. But the audience recognizes that Ann, as a vital female, embodies this Life Force—Shaw's name for a creative principle in the universe which promises to evolve ordinary humanity (man) into an ever more powerful species (superman) by bringing together the right combination of male and female, whether they like it or not. The Life Force, however, does not always succeed. Sometimes male resists female and leaves her to spend her vitality in less glorious enterprises than the creation of the superman. This is how the conflict is resolved in *Pygmalion,* at least in its original ending. (Subsequent film and musical comedy versions broadly hint that Higgins and Eliza stay together.) Eliza Doolittle, a flower girl, becomes a lady by learning to speak proper English. But being a lady, she learns, is a lot like being a doll, and when her speech teacher, Henry Higgins, gets tired of playing with her, she finds that she is worse off than when she started. She can't go back to the gutter now that she has the habits and tastes of a lady. And she has no standing in Higgins' life and household because they are not married and Higgins is a determined bachelor. Although Higgins believes that Eliza will accept this ambiguous situation, the audience knows that he is blind to what is in her heart: the need for recognition and the desire to be treated as a human being, not an object. Like Ibsen's Nora, she walks out on the imperceptive male as the curtain falls.

Readers interested in the male-female conflict need not confine themselves to the dramas of Ibsen, Strindberg, and Shaw. Both the destructive and creative aspects of this struggle continue to be presented by playwrights in our own time. In a lighter vein, English playwright Noel Coward explores the battle of the sexes in such works as his comedy *Private Lives,* as does Edward Albee, more painfully, in *Who's Afraid of Virginia Woolf?* The singer-heroine of Gretchen Cryer's *I'm Getting My Act Together and Taking It on the Road* does what the title says when she finds that her husband-producer will not accept her desire to change her show business image to match her real self. In Ntozake Shange's *for colored girls who have considered suicide/when the rainbow is enuf,* a chorus of young women, all bearing emotional scars from their relationships with men, resolve their conflicts through profound self-recognition, declaring, "i found god in myself & i loved her/i loved her fiercely."

The Individual vs. Society

As the author of two scandalous plays about marriage, *A Doll's House* and *Ghosts,* Ibsen found himself under attack from conservative and idealist factions. His response to this attack was a play called *An Enemy of the People.* Dr. Thomas Stockmann, the protagonist, discovers that the supposedly curative waters of a local health resort are actually full of industrial pollution. When he attempts to correct the situation, he is told by his brother, the Mayor, to suppress his report because the town cannot afford to detoxify the water. Dr. Stockmann nevertheless attempts to publicize the unsafe conditions. But community leaders, whose prosperity depends on the resort, block his efforts and, at a public meeting, declare him an enemy of the people because he is threatening the economic growth of the town. Stockmann emerges from the meeting vowing to fight on. Flanked by his wife and daughter, amid glass and rubble from stones "the people" have thrown through his windows, he declares, "The strongest man is he who stands most alone."

In the United States, Arthur Miller has produced several versions of this conflict between the truth-seeking individual and a lying and corrupt society. In *All My Sons* Chris Keller discovers that his father, Joe, has indirectly caused American war casualties by knowingly selling defective airplane parts to the military during World War II. Joe's defense is the profit motive: "Nothin's clean. It's dollars and cents [in] war and peace." When he learns, however, that his other son has killed himself because he could not bear the shame of what his father did, he takes his own life. In 1950, Miller adapted Ibsen's *An Enemy of the People* for American audiences and, in 1953, again dramatized the struggle of one man against society in *The Crucible,* set in Salem, Massachusetts, during the witchcraft trials of 1692. The protagonist, John Proctor, is wrongly accused of witchcraft and refuses to sign his name to a faked confession. The judge explains that the "crime" will be forgiven if he signs, but that he will be hanged if he doesn't. Proctor still refuses: "Because it is my name. Because I cannot have another in my life. . . . How may I live without my name?" Miller faced something like Proctor's dilemma in real life (without the prospect of a hanging, fortunately) when he refused to inform on fellow writers during an appearance before the House Committee on Un-American Activities in 1956.*

Shaw, also a champion of social justice in real life, dramatized social issues in most of his plays. In fact, his handling of the battle of the sexes usually

---

*Miller's refusal prompted Molly Kazan, whose husband, Elia, had cooperated with the committee, to write a play called *The Egghead* in which the stand-alone protagonist turns out to be wrong and society right.

involves the reader in political and economic aspects of the situation. This elaboration of male-female conflict culminated in *Saint Joan*. After saving France and its helpless male leaders from the English through heroic and even miraculous military exploits, the young Frenchwoman finds herself in serious trouble with two major social establishments of her day: the Catholic Church and militaristic feudalism. Joan has made the mistake of asserting her right to live according to personal inspiration rather than the dictates of male-dominated social institutions. Realizing that this heresy can (and did, historically) destroy their absolute power, Joan's enemies threaten to excommunicate her and burn her at the stake. Her final recognition is the same as John Proctor's; she cannot affix her name to a false confession, even though the Archbishop assures her that it will save her soul. She goes to her death because she believes in what she calls her "voices" more than in the institutions which claim authority over her.

Shaw departs from the realistic method of the first six scenes of *Saint Joan* and ends the play with an epilogue in which Joan, along with other major characters, appears in a vision to Charles II, the man she crowned King of France. During Charles' vision, a visitor from the future announces (to everyone's delight) that Joan has been made a saint. When she offers to return to earth, however, it's a different story; the characters hastily apologize and disappear as Charles goes back to sleep. The conflict between the free and vital individual and the limiting effects of human society is now seen in its cosmic dimension. Left alone with the audience to ponder this, Joan prays, "O God that madest this beautiful earth, when will it be ready to receive thy saints? How long, O Lord, how long?" Wishing to expand the play's field of conflict to include the cosmos, Shaw moves his point of view beyond realism into the realm of the visionary.

Humanity vs. the Mystery of Life

In *Man and Superman* and *Saint Joan,* Shaw supplements his realistic images of life as it is, with images from the realm of dreams and visions. This desire to penetrate the mystery of life has, as we have said, led many playwrights to abandon realism altogether and invent new kinds of dramatic imagery. Images of life as it is are replaced or supplemented by images of life as it *really* is, beneath the surface or from the perspective of history or eternity. We examine this antirealistic effort more closely in the next chapter. We should note here, however, that a number of primarily realistic modern plays do attempt to deal directly with the struggle to understand the significance of human life in a universal context. Two examples are Thornton Wilder's *Our Town* and Eugene O'Neill's *The Iceman Cometh*.

The *mise en scène* of *Our Town* is unusual. Although Wilder presents ordinary people doing the usual things of daily life, the setting of the play is a bare stage. As in classical drama, the background of each scene is described by a choruslike character, the Stage Manager. The illusion of life as it is, is created without scenery and with a minimum of props. A few chairs, a ladder, and, for the funeral scene, a number of open umbrellas are about all that is required. Other objects are suggested in pantomime. Lighting and costumes are the primary visual elements. By stripping away the usual details of realistic settings, Wilder asks the reader to imagine both the fictional behavior of the characters and the bare walls of the stage. While the characters live in the imaginary world of the play, the Stage Manager inhabits the real world of the theatre and the audience.

The play is written in three acts. The Stage Manager tells us that the first act is called Daily Life and the second Love and Marriage, leaving us to guess at the title of Act III, set in a cemetery (Birth and Death?). Several of the play's characters have died and sit in rows of chairs waiting for whatever comes next. Emily Webb, a young woman who has just died in childbirth, wants to go back and relive her past. She chooses the day of her twelfth birthday. But real life, seen from the perspective of death, turns out to be unbearably beautiful, and living people are sadly unaware of its beauty. Before long, Emily asks to return to her grave, and her wish is granted. The Stage Manager, who has apparently been through all this before, looks at the stars, winds his watch, and sends the audience home to bed.

Emily wants to realize every minute of her life as it is, as she lives it. But this is only possible from the perspective of death. The Stage Manager, presiding over this conflict, concludes that perhaps only saints and poets can overcome the obstacles which stand in Emily's way. But there are no saints or poets in Our Town. In the resolution, the reader may detect an invitation to choose between going on in the usual blind way or becoming a saint or a poet.

The mise en scène of O'Neill's The Iceman Cometh is totally realistic. The setting is the back room bar of Harry Hope's saloon and flophouse in New York in 1912. The cast of characters includes Harry, his two bartenders, three prostitutes, and ten assorted roomers. A number of these characters are on the stage most of the time, in various degrees of alcoholic stupor, waiting for the next free drink. While waiting, they indulge their favorite pipe dreams: Harry Hope, who has not left the saloon since his wife died, will take a walk around the neighborhood "someday"; Rocky, who manages the streetwalkers, is a bartender, not a pimp, and the girls are not whores, only tarts; Jimmy Tomorrow will get his old job back—tomorrow; Joe Mott, a black, believes he is really white; even Larry Slade's "waiting for death" pose masks a pitiful clinging to life at any cost.

The occasion of the play is the upcoming birthday party of the group's hero, Hickey, a traveling salesman. Their lives seem to center on Hickey. They tell affectionate tales of his drinking habits, of his sayings and stories, and they look forward eagerly to his yearly birthday visit. Most of all, they count on Hickey to support them in their pipe dreams. But this time there is something wrong, and something new, which threatens to destroy this world in miniature. No sooner has Hickey arrived than he declares that he has quit drinking. And worse—he announces that he is going to bring them deep spiritual peace by curing each and every one of them of their pipe dreams. Listening in pained disbelief, the "chorus" of derelicts beg Hickey to stop talking, to be the old Hickey, to leave them with their illusions, and let them get drunk in peace.

This conflict between the reality-bearing Hickey and the illusion-thirsty chorus takes an unexpected twist when Hickey reveals that he has killed his wife, Evelyn, and, in so doing, destroyed his own pipe dream—the massive lie that their marriage was an idyllic feast of love. At the climax, even Hickey cannot face the truth of his life and invents a new lie to resolve the situation: Hickey discovers he is insane and has been so since he arrived. The chorus join in, pretending they knew it all along. As Hickey is hauled away by the police, the booze regains its kick, the pipe dream its power, and life is restored to the saloon. As the setting fades into darkness, everyone begins to sing—a different song for each character. In *The Iceman Cometh*, each life must be maintained by a pipe dream. Reality is too much for the human race.

To achieve their particular cosmic visions, both *Our Town* and *The Iceman Cometh* make use of devices from classical drama. In *Our Town* the dramatic space includes the theatre and the audience, and the Stage Manager functions in somewhat the same way as a Shakespearean prologue or chorus. The action of the play unfolds against a permanent and timeless background, rather than in a specific environment. The bare stage stands for the universe, and the characters' behavior becomes universal human behavior. In *The Iceman Cometh*, the roomful of derelicts represents a complete community. Like the chorus of a Greek tragedy, their fate is directly tied to the protagonist's—his conflict is their conflict. Hickey acts not only for himself, but for them and, by implication, for all humanity. The action of both *Our Town* and *The Iceman Cometh* is presented in a public, not a private, forum and can therefore be more easily viewed as an image of the struggle of all humankind to solve the mystery of life.

Personal Dream vs. the Real World

A great deal of modern drama emphasizes neither sexual, social, political, nor cosmic conflicts. In many realistic plays ordinary individuals struggle against the realities of their limited worlds to achieve a personal dream. Sometimes these realities are at least temporarily overcome, the protagonist enjoys a momentary victory, and hope for the future is offered in the resolution. This happens in *A Raisin in the Sun*, when Walter Younger leads his family out of their Chicago tenement into an unknown but promising future. More usually, however, the protagonist's objectives turn out to be what O'Neill's Hickey calls a pipe dream.

American drama is especially rich in pipe dream conflicts. In Clifford Odets' *Paradise Lost*, a New York family laments the disappearance of deeply cherished ideals. The hero of his *Golden Boy* regrets having traded his violin for boxing gloves. The Arab, a prophetic character in William Saroyan's *The Time of Your Life,* sees that human aspiration is baseless as he concludes, "No foundation, all the way down the line." In Tennessee Williams' *The Glass Menagerie,* the autobiographical hero, Tom, is caught between the faded pipe dreams of his mother and sister and a real world which is "lit by lightning." Williams' *A Streetcar Named Desire* develops this conflict further in vividly contrasting characters; Blanche DuBois covers the naked light bulb of her sister's shabby flat with a paper lantern and affects the genteel behavior of a long-gone past, while her brutal brother-in-law, Stanley Kowalski, flings raw meat about the stage and at last drives Blanche from his home into a mental institution. Arthur Miller's *Death of a Salesman* dramatizes the last desperate hours of a burned-out salesman, who clings in vain to his fantasy of a world in which his business triumphs and those of his son take on almost godlike proportions. The act of facing reality is fraught with such suffering that Willy chooses suicide rather than part with what Miller calls his "massive dreams." In *The Crucible,* Miller reverses the process. The protagonist, John Proctor, finds himself to be one of the few undeluded members of his community, where a witch-hunt is transforming the real world into a nightmare from which the only awakening is death. In O'Neill's *Long Day's Journey Into Night,* the four members of the Tyrone family have become so addicted to their pipe dreams that any attempt to speak the truth produces unbearable anguish. The protagonist of John Guare's *The House of Blue Leaves* is so hopelessly in love with the idea of media stardom that he fails to recognize he is also a hopelessly untalented songwriter. Sam Shepard produced two plays of American family life, *The Curse of the Starving Class* and *Buried Child,* in which individual family members seem hypnotized by personal illusions and oblivious to the reality of others. In Shepard's drama, the very existence of a real world is in question; illusion may be all there is. For this reason, and others, it will be helpful to consider his plays further in the context of antirealism.

Of the many modern dramatists who have investigated this conflict between personal dreams and the real world—including Ibsen in *The Wild Duck* and Shaw in *Heartbreak House*—none has done so more consistently or penetratingly than Anton Chekhov. In his four major full-length plays, the reader will find an infinitely varied, sharply observed, and compassionate exploration of one central action: human yearning. Although there is more than one kind of behavior in Chekhov's drama, yearning is the main action of his major characters. In *The Sea Gull* they yearn for an all-enfolding love; in *Uncle Vanya,* for freedom and release from duty; in *The Three Sisters,* for rebirth and a new life; and in *The Cherry Orchard,* for home. The obstacle in each case—life as it is. The very action of yearning blinds Chekhov's characters to reality. The conflict changes shape, tone, and direction but is never resolved. To express this ever-changing yet never-changing situation, Chekhov created mosaic, rather than linear, dramatic structures.

Mosaic Realism

For the most part, the plays discussed so far in this chapter can be read as linear drama. Each of the four macroconflicts is expressed through a protagonist who struggles against obstacles in pursuit of an objective, faces some kind of truth, and resolves the situation for the world of the play. Even *Our Town,* which contains many actions and climaxes, has a protagonist, Emily Webb, who faces a truth—the full realization of life is not available to ordinary mortals—which is shared by other characters. In reading the plays of Chekhov, however, we should be prepared for something different. Although his plays contain the familiar dramatic elements of conflict and recognition, plot and character, and resolution and meaning, they are arranged in nonlinear, or mosaic, patterns.

The first act of *The Sea Gull,* for instance, is full of conflict. But instead of building steadily toward a climax, these conflicts are all variations on one theme: yearning for something—mostly love—which is unattainable. This yearning comes full circle when Masha, vainly pursued by the lovelorn Medvedenko, expresses her unrequited love for Treplev. What's more, Masha clings to her hopeless love to the end of the play and beyond, through marriage to Medvedenko and motherhood, without ever telling Treplev. And this hidden love is but one thread in a tapestry of similar longings. Because hidden truths are rarely faced, fully developed recognition is elusive, and the characters remain caught in their private situations. Although they share many common occasions, each has a separate and hidden idea of "what's wrong?" Rather than look for an emerging showdown, then, the reader is better advised to understand, first of all, the setting and the situation—where the characters are and what they are doing. Once these circumstances are clearly in mind, we can see how the occasion serves to hide each character's personal situation from the others, and even from himself. This, and not a buildup to a climax, is the source of dramatic tension.

In *The Sea Gull,* the occasions revolve around the comings and goings of Irina Nikolayevna Arkadina, an actress. The play is set in various parts of the country estate belonging to her brother, Sorin. When Irina visits the estate between theatrical engagements, she is treated as a celebrity. In Act I, it is a summer evening and an outdoor stage has been set up on the lawn. Irina's son, Treplev, is presenting a play he has written, hoping to impress his mother. Act II takes place on another part of the lawn on a summer afternoon, where members of the family are passing the time talking and reading. A long-standing feud between Irina and the foreman of the estate breaks out, and Irina threatens to leave but later changes her mind. A week later, in Act III, she has changed her mind again and is in the process of leaving. The setting is the dining room, which is full of her trunks and boxes. Act IV takes place one windy autumn evening two years later. Irina has just arrived for a visit, and her socializing spills into the drawing room which her son sometimes uses as a study.

Mosaic of Conflicts in Act I of The Sea Gull

Medvedenko wants to share his love with Masha,
but she is indifferent.

Sorin wants to leave the estate,
but he has nowhere to go.

Treplev wants his mother's attention,
but she is self-centered.

Treplev wants to love Nina,
but she is preoccupied with
other thoughts.

Polina wants to love Dorn,
but he is indifferent.

Shamraev wants to enjoy
great theatre, but he
believes there is none left.

Treplev wants to impress
his mother, but she is
disdainful.

Sorin wants Irina to respect
Treplev's feelings, but she is
offended by her son's play.

Irina wants to make up
with Treplev, but he runs
away.

Nina wants to stay,
but her father
expects her home.

Sorin wants the dog
untied, but Shamraev
refuses.

Dorn wants to encourage Treplev
in his writing, but Treplev is
preoccupied with Nina.

Masha wants to love Treplev,
but he is focused on his mother.

In Chekhov's method of plotting there is no single character on whose fate the world of the play is centered. Instead, he presents an ensemble of characters, each of whom is a unique expression of the central theme. Notice the meshing of conflicts in the above chart.

Since the occasions in *The Sea Gull* revolve around Irina, is she not the protagonist? Not if by protagonist we mean a character whose objectives generate persistent actions directed against resistant obstacles. There is no sense of striving or struggle in Irina's character, beyond trying to maintain her youthful image. And Treplev, although he does act to remove obstacles, is not the protagonist either, if by protagonist we mean a character whose action touches the fate of all other characters in the world of the play. Irina's behavior provides the basic occasion of each act. Treplev's behavior is the result of tension between these occasions and his private situation. Since occasion and setting, rather than situation, are in the foreground, the plot in Chekhov can be said to be organized around an *ensemble,* or group of characters, rather than a single protagonist.

These settings and occasions, furthermore, are not linked to one another in any cause-and-effect sequence. They simply represent typical moments in the characters' lives, as they relate to Irina's presence or absence. The behavior of the characters is keyed to each particular setting and occasion, with no momentous situation brewing in which everyone has a crucial stake. This is what Chekhov meant by "people as they are, not on stilts." When private situations do erupt, they break the surface of the occasion only momentarily. Mostly, life goes on as it always has. Only the reader is in a position to discover how these characters' private desires resonate with one another in tune with a common theme. For the reader, the dramatic tension is released in this series of discoveries. As the images of the play accumulate, we watch an emerging vision of human yearning in all its facets—sad, funny, and mysterious.

The reader's role in the release of dramatic tension in Chekhov is clearly evident in the climaxes and resolutions of *Hedda Gabler* and *The Sea Gull* (see Script 7, p. 50). As we read Ibsen's drama, Hedda herself emerges clearly as the protagonist. We see the other characters through her eyes. Their actions are significant insofar as they affect her. When Hedda commits suicide at the climax of the play, her action has an explosive effect on all the other characters. Tesman loses his decorative wife, Judge Brack a potential mistress, and Mrs. Elvsted a feared rival. Berta, the long-suffering servant, shares the horror of the other onlookers. As readers, we are witnesses not only to Hedda's deed but to its effect on the world of the play, now assembled in the dramatic space. The tension of Hedda's struggle is released and a new world, a new future, is constituted in the Tesman household.

Rather than an explosion, Treplev's suicide at the end of *The Sea Gull* produces what we might call an implosion—an inward bursting which has only a limited impact on the world of the play. Although there are seven characters in the dramatic space, only Dr. Dorn and Trigorin know what has happened. The resolution of the play deals, not with Treplev's situation, but with an adjustment of the occasion—"Get Irina Nikolayevna away from here." What is important, in the world of the play, is not that the mother should recognize at last who her son was and what he has done, but that she should be protected from anything new or wrong. In a sense, the objective of the ensemble is to preserve the occasion against the explosive consequences of emerging situations. Treplev's situation, which no one but the reader has fully recognized, has been resolved in death.

This tendency can also be seen in the action of *The Cherry Orchard*. The primary situation is that the family estate, the home the characters all yearn for, is about to be sold for unpaid taxes. A secondary situation is that neither of the young women of the family has been provided with a husband—an important social necessity in the world of this play. Yet another situation is that the eighty-seven-year-old servant, Firs, is seriously ill. Responsibility for all of these problems lies with Lyubov Andreyevna, owner of the estate, mother of the girls, and head of the household. Lyubov's objective is not to solve these problems but to manage the various occasions which the estate has traditionally supported: a joyful homecoming from an unhappy life in Paris; a leisurely afternoon with friends in a meadow on the estate; a dancing party for the family and the neighbors; and a tearful leave-taking, together with a perfunctory last-minute effort to arrange a proposal for one of the girls, as members of the family bid sentimental farewell to the cherry orchard and go their separate ways. The estate is sold, the girls face an uncertain future, and Firs dies, forgotten, in the empty nursery. But the occasions go on without significant interruption.

One possible exception to this rule occurs in the third act, during the dancing party, which has been scheduled to take place at the same time that the estate is being auctioned off. "It was the wrong time to give a ball," Lyubov admits. "But never mind," she adds as she sits and hums to the music. A halfhearted effort has been made to raise some money to save the estate but it seems doomed to failure. In the middle of the party the real estate developer Lopahin, a friend of the family, bursts in with the news that *he* has bought the estate. It was this same Lopahin who had warned Lyubov of the danger she was in and had offered a plan to save the estate, by creating and selling subdivisions. But this plan was the kind of new occasion Lyubov was not prepared to understand. "Why didn't you listen to me?" Lopahin asks her, as she weeps at the news and the orchestra plays on in the background. "And now it's too late, there's no turning back." The economics of Lopahin's business dictate that the cherry orchard be cut down, the old house razed, and summer cottages be erected to assure a profit.

Lopahin's purchase of the cherry orchard is not the result of a persistent objective. It comes about almost by accident, in the course of an occasion familiar to Lopahin—an estate auction. The plot of *The Cherry Orchard* does not center on a conflict between a family struggling to keep their home and an unscrupulous real estate dealer. (This *is* the conflict in a number of modern plays. An example is Sam Shepard's *The Curse of the Starving Class*.) Lopahin could have saved the estate if the family had been capable of understanding their situation. The world had changed and large estates were no longer economically viable. No one even remembers how to harvest and market the fruit of the cherry trees. Lopahin, too, is in the grip of new economic forces and is as astonished as everyone else that he is now the owner of the estate where his father was a serf.

In this chapter, we surveyed modern realism from the point of view of four macroconflicts. By macroconflict we mean, in this case, a very general conflict which recurs in a large group of plays taken as a whole. An awareness of these can provide a basic sense of direction when encountering any of these plays for the first time. To make a strong connection with the dramatic action of a specific play, however, nothing takes the place of a lively imagination, a receptive empathy, and those analytical skills which can uncover the specific, moment-to-moment conflict of the drama at hand. The characters of realistic drama do not behave in terms of macroconflicts but out of a persistent need to overcome specific resistance to their visions of the future, just as we do every day. "Life is strife," says a character in Gertrude Stein's *The Mother of Us All*, "and every day I give my life." The everyday giving and receiving of life is the basic stuff of realistic drama.

16 ❧ Antirealism

NINA: It's difficult to act in your play. There
are no real-life characters in it.
TREPLEV: Real-life characters! We have to show
life not as it is, not as it should be, but as it
appears in our dreams.

—*The Sea Gull*

We have seen, in the preceding chapter, that it is possible
to use one of four major conflicts as a starting point in reading realistic drama.
Antirealistic drama, too, can be read from this perspective. But such an approach would not help us discover what makes antirealism different from
realism. To make this difference clear, we now focus on the various kinds of
awareness which antirealistic drama stimulates in the reader, whatever the
conflict.

Realistic images of action appeal to our ordinary consciousness of life as it
is. By reading realistic plays, we connect with the everyday behavior of
ordinary people in familiar settings. The scope of this behavior is limited by the
particular language, customs, manners, and socioeconomic circumstances
which prevail in the world of the play. Allowing for historical and cultural
differences, we can say that the images of realism are presented to the reader in
the same terms we use to present ourselves to one another in daily life.

But, as we all know, there is more to life than the everyday routine and
more to consciousness than our ordinary thoughts and feelings. As social
human beings we continually confirm for one another our share in a common,
but limited, reality. As private individuals we also inhabit a larger world of
hopes, fears, fantasies, and visions which shape our behavior and our view of
common reality. Antirealistic drama offers us a way of exploring this intangible, but vitally important, world.

How can we understand dramatic action which extends beyond our ordinary consciousness of life as it is? It depends on which direction the playwright
chooses to take us. Some plays delve beneath the surface into the irrational and
symbolic world of dreams. Others invite us to inspect the hidden mechanisms
of social morality. Still others climb the heights of metaphysical speculation.
Whereas realistic drama is akin to psychology and sociology, antirealism has
affinities with religion and philosophy. (We have already seen, in chapter 15,
how realists like Shaw resort to antirealistic devices when they wish to extend
the dramatic action into the philosophic realm.) But whatever the direction,

antirealism seeks always to free us from the limitations of private reality and show us our lives in a wider and more timeless perspective.

The continuing oscillation between realism and antirealism in the theatre of the past hundred years has produced many movements and countermovements, together with a long list of exotic brand names including Theatre of Cruelty, Theatre of the Grotesque, Theatre of Panic, Ontological-Hysteric Theatre, and Theatre of the Ridiculous. Some of these movements have produced new kinds of drama, while others are better known for provocative performance theory or novel approaches to the *mise en scène*. We cannot hope, in an introductory survey, to cover every variation on the theme of antirealism. For the sake of clarity we focus, instead, on three major modern traditions: expressionistic drama, Brechtian drama, and absurdist drama. The fourth and final section of this chapter examines antirealism in recent American drama.

Expressionistic Drama

Arthur Miller's *Death of a Salesman* presents the life of Willy Loman from outside and inside perspectives. We see Willy as his family and neighbors see him. But we are also shown "the inside of his head" in fragments of memory and in the hallucinatory visitations of his brother, Ben. This view from the inside is called *expressionism* because it expresses a private state of mind which is not shared with other characters. We can say, then, that *Death of a Salesman* has a realistic framework but contains expressionistic elements.

Strindberg's *The Ghost Sonata,* by contrast, is almost wholly expressionistic. Strindberg shows us the inside of someone's head without showing us the outside. Reading this play is very much like being in someone else's dream, but without the framework of that individual's reality. A number of commentators have tried to supply a realistic framework for this, and other, Strindbergian drama by matching the dramatic images with incidents from the author's life. But, unless we are experts, this kind of study may distract us from the immediate experience of the play. Although *The Ghost Sonata* is undeniably subjective, we can still connect with its mysterious imagery. One way to do this is to become more aware of our own dream life.

Some people are fascinated by their dreams, while others claim they never dream, or, if they do, they never remember *what* they dream. In either case dreaming, like anything else, can be improved with practice. One way to do this is to keep a dream diary. The struggle to translate dream imagery into language brings out the difference between the subjective and shifting nature of dreams and the comparative objectivity and fixity of language. The dream may change and parts of it may dissolve, as it is put into words. But the effort of keeping a dream diary can increase awareness of the way expressionistic drama works.

Another fruitful approach to dreams is to look at each dream element as a fragment of our own personality. Since we are the creators of our dreams, every part of the dream, from people and objects to colors and sounds, is a part of ourselves. Connecting with all aspects of the dream is very much like reading drama by empathizing with every character. In *The Ghost Sonata*, the reader is invited to feel and think like an apparition, a mummy, and a vampire—among other characters from the dreamlike world of this play. By doing this, we become the dreamer of the drama and begin to experience its meaning from the inside. This meaning is likely to be highly personal and difficult to share with others, which is the kind of experience the expressionistic playwright tries to dramatize in the first place.

But expressionistic drama is never wholly subjective. As in all drama, there are familiar structural elements. The plot of an expressionistic play, for instance, may be mosaic or linear. *A Dream Play* and *The Ghost Sonata* have predominantly mosaic plots. On the other hand, Strindberg's American admirer Eugene O'Neill created a more linear expressionism in such works as *The Emperor Jones* and *The Hairy Ape*. A brief comparison of *The Ghost Sonata* with *The Emperor Jones* will illustrate the difference.

Although there is conflict in *The Ghost Sonata*, it is not sustained in a clear cause-and-effect pattern. The Old Man **wants** the Student to marry his daughter (the Girl) **but** his objective is prevented when the Mummy exposes his crimes in scene 2. This recognition of the Old Man's true character transforms him into a grotesque, parrotlike creature who takes the Mummy's place in the closet and dies there. The Student also **wants** to marry the Girl **but** she, too, dies mysteriously in the final scene. The obstacles in each conflict appear to be supernatural, since neither the Old Man nor the Girl dies of natural causes.

The action of *The Ghost Sonata* is not generated by conflict so much as by the tension between the natural occasions of life and an underlying supernatural situation. In the first scene a chance encounter in the street between the Student and the Old Man,—who once knew the Student's father, is haunted by the apparition of a drowning girl (the Milkmaid). The family gathering in scene 2 is actually a "ghost supper" in which the Old Man is revealed as Hummel, the vampire. As the Student is courting the Girl in scene 3, she announces that she is dying and calls for the death screen, which was placed around Hummel in scene 2. Human life on the natural plane seems out of harmony with supernatural laws relating to good and evil. And, although the Student is a "Sunday child," that is, someone who can see beyond the limits of everyday reality, he is unable to do anything but comment on the situation. As the play ends, the real world is replaced by an image of the world of the dead where, perhaps, some resolution is to be found. For those of us on this side of the grave, however, the play presents a sequence of unresolved and contradictory dream images of the continuing human struggle with issues of sin and redemption.

By contrast, in the eight scenes of O'Neill's *The Emperor Jones*, a mounting conflict leads to a climax, just before the final curtain, in which the underlying situation is completely resolved. The protagonist is Brutus Jones, a black American who has made himself the emperor of a small island in the

Parallel Worlds in The Ghost Sonata

Role	*Foreground World*	*Shadow World*
husband	The Colonel	The Caretaker
wife	The Mummy	The Caretaker's Wife
wife's lover	The Old Man	The Dead Man
illegitimate daughter of the wife and her lover	The Girl	The Lady in Black
daughter's lover	The Student	The Aristocrat

The cast of characters of *The Ghost Sonata* consists of two ensembles, the second a kind of shadow version of the first. These worlds exist side by side, subtly reflecting one another, but do not converge in the course of the dramatic action. After the Old Man dies, the Student refers to him as "the dead man," suggesting that the characters may be moving through different worlds which, nevertheless, resemble one another. The Old Man seems to sense this when he tells the Student, "My life is like a book of fairy tales. And though the stories are different, they're held together by a common thread, and the main theme constantly recurs." This kind of thematic repetition is characteristic of mosaic plots.

West Indies. In the first scene we learn that the emperor's subjects are mounting a revolution against him. Jones is confident that he can escape from the island and live out his life on what he has stolen from the natives. But he does not reckon with the destructive psychological effects of fear and panic. Just as he is boasting about how superior he is to his pursuers, an ominous sound is heard:

> [*From the distant hills comes the faint, steady thump of a tom-tom, low and vibrating. It starts at a rate exactly corresponding to normal pulse beat—72 to the minute—and continues at a gradually accelerating rate from this point uninterruptedly to the very end of the play.*]

During the next 6 scenes this drumbeat gradually strips Jones of his sanity, as he tries to find his way through the jungle to safety. First, he encounters the Little Formless Fears—"black, shapeless, only their glittering eyes can be seen." Then he has a series of hallucinations about a man he has murdered, a slave auction in which he himself is on the block, and, finally, a terrifying encounter with a Congo witch doctor. In the final scene Jones has been tracked down by the revolutionaries, who kill him with a fusillade of silver bullets.

When Jones dies, the sound of the tom-tom suddenly stops. After this journey into madness, seen from the inside of Jones' head, we are returned, at the final curtain, to the real world, as the other characters gather around his corpse.

A linear plot, tracing the inner feelings of a protagonist on his way to destruction, is also used in such expressionistic plays as O'Neill's *The Hairy Ape* and *From Morn to Midnight* by German playwright Georg Kaiser. But whether linear or mosaic in method, expressionistic drama challenges us, as readers, to explore the world of the irrational, the supernatural, and the subconscious.

The Drama of Bertolt Brecht

Not all antirealistic drama is set in the realm of the subconscious. In the plays of Bertolt Brecht we learn to extend our consciousness in the opposite direction, toward a more rational awareness of the connection between the choices we make in our personal lives and the social forces and institutions we accept as inevitable. Conflict between the individual and society, seen in the work of a number of realists, is also present in Brecht's plays. His method, however, is unique. We will not find, in most of his scripts, that sustained presentation of observed reality found in the pages of Ibsen, Shaw, and Arthur Miller. Instead, Brecht deliberately and openly re-creates reality in a way that challenges our assumptions about life as it is. His images of action are intended to rearrange rather than reproduce our usual and familiar view of the world.

Brecht's scripts have more in common with Shakespeare's than with Ibsen's. Like Shakespeare, Brecht was involved in many aspects of theatrical creation. In addition to writing plays, Brecht worked as a teacher, director, producer, adapter, and prolific writer of dramatic theory. His scripts are more like works-in-progress than the finished "books" of Ibsen. His stage directions, for instance, contain no meticulously conceived dramatic space but only the briefest indication of setting. "We often begin rehearsing without any knowledge of stage design," he said of his method of work with designer Caspar Neher. The reader of a Brecht script is more likely to feel he is attending a rehearsal than a finished performance.

Although Brecht did create a unique *mise en scène* for each of his plays, it performs a different function than in plays of "fourth wall" realism. Brecht does not use the *mise en scène* to transport us across a mystic chasm into a world of illusion. Instead, he asks us to remain aware that the theatre event is a created reality which results from conscious artistic choices. In production, Brecht achieved this effect by exposing the mechanisms of the theatre for the audience to see. The pieces of scenery looked like pieces of scenery; the magic of electricity was demystified by leaving lighting instruments fully visible; the fictional situations and occasions of the play were spelled out on large signs above the actors; and the action was regularly interrupted by songs and choric

Opening Stage Directions from the Plays of Bertolt Brecht

Mother Courage (English version by Eric Bentley)
[*Spring, 1624. In Dalarna, the Swedish Commander Oxenstierna is recruiting for the campaign in Poland. The canteen woman Anna Fierling, commonly known as* MOTHER COURAGE, *loses a son. Highway outside a town. A* SERGEANT *and a* RECRUITING OFFICER *stand shivering.*]

The Good Woman of Setzuan (English version by Eric Bentley)
[*At the gates of the half-Westernized city of Setzuan. Evening.* WONG *the Water Seller introduces himself to the audience.*]

Life of Galileo (translated by Wolfgang Sauerlander and Ralph Manheim)
[*Galileo Galilei, teacher of mathematics in Padua, sets out to demonstrate the new Copernican system.*
In the year sixteen hundred and nine
Science's light began to shine.
At Padua city, in a modest house
Galileo Galilei set out to prove
The sun is still, the earth is on the move.]

The stage directions of a Brecht script provide occasion and situation as well as setting. In *Mother Courage* we learn at once that the protagonist will lose one of her sons in the war. This foreknowledge sheds a special light on the action to come by making us more aware than the characters of the consequences of their choices. It also offers us a chance to think of alternative choices. *The Good Woman of Setzuan* begins with a very brief indication of setting and a direct address to the audience, as in many Shakespearean scripts. Here, and throughout the play, Brecht does not attempt to create the illusion that we are in a Chinese city. Like the play-within-the-play in *The Caucasian Chalk Circle, The Good Woman of Setzuan* seems to be, instead, "a very old Chinese play that has a bearing on our problem." The opening words of the script of *Life of Galileo* are intended to be projected on a screen for the audience to read, as are many of Brecht's opening stage directions. The projections remind us that we are about to be told a story that takes place "once upon a time." Since there is usually more than one way to tell a story, we are made aware, as the drama begins, of the storyteller's power to create new realities.

commentary to prevent the audience from becoming hypnotized by the action. Brecht used this method, called *epic theatre,* to remind the audience that the world we live in is also, like the theatre, a created reality, and that this reality can also be changed by making conscious choices. Just as theatre artists create fictional societies, so theatre audiences create real societies. Brecht's drama is meant to expose the mechanisms of this process, just as his *mise en scène* exposes the mechanisms of the theatre.

In many Brechtian conflicts, the protagonist wants to live happily without harming others, and maybe even do some good in the world. (Mack the Knife, in *The Threepenny Opera,* can only live happily by harming others.) But the world does not work that way. Instead, in the world as it really is, people can only stay alive by exploiting one another or by denying their own goodness. In *Mother Courage,* the protagonist makes her living off the war, which eventually destroys the children she is struggling to raise. In *The Good Woman of Setzuan,* the prostitute, Shen Te, wants to lead a decent life, but her goodness is continually taken advantage of by the needy townspeople. The scientist, in the *Life of Galileo,* discovers important truths and wants to deliver them to humanity, but the Inquisition regards his discoveries as heresy and threatens him with death. In *The Caucasion Chalk Circle,* the kitchen maid, Grusha, by taking pity on and adopting the infant child of a deposed ruler, exposes herself to prolonged hardship and danger and almost loses the man she loves. In these and other plays, the protagonist's survival is threatened by overwhelming social and historical forces. Brecht structures the conflict in such a way that the only lasting resolution would be to change the world.

This kind of conflict is also found in such plays as Shaw's *Saint Joan* and Arthur Miller's *The Crucible.* In these plays, however, the focus is on whether or not the protagonist will maintain a heroic integrity in the face of hostile social institutions. For Brecht, such heroism was futile if it did not help to change society. The action of his plays is intended to give the audience rather than the protagonist a chance to recognize this truth. In his notes on *Mother Courage* Brecht wrote:

> It is not incumbent on the playwright to give Mother Courage insight at the end—she sees something, around the middle of the play, at the close of the sixth scene, then loses again what she has seen—his concern is that the spectator should see.

To help the spectator recognize the truth of the situation, Brecht creates another dimension of action, partly with the epic theatre style of *mise en scène,* and partly through choric behavior. In *The Threepenny Opera,* for instance, the main characters divide their time almost equally between a frenzied struggle to survive and stepping out of character to share insights into their desperate condition. At the end of the first act, Mr. Peachum, Bible in hand, sings these words:

The right to happiness is fundamental:
Men live so little time and die alone.
Nor is it altogether accidental
That they want bread to eat and not a stone.
The right to happiness is fundamental.
And yet how great would be the innovation
Should someone claim and get the right—hooray!
The thought appeals to my imagination!
But this old world of ours ain't built that way.

But, although he helps us to recognize the situation, Peachum is completely in its power when in character. In spite of his interest in the Bible, he, like everyone else in the play, lives by exploiting others. If we, as audience members, are tempted to respond, Then why don't you *do* something about it? we find we are talking to ourselves. This device of making the audience, rather than the protagonist, responsible for facing the truth can be seen even more clearly in *The Good Woman of Setzuan*. Unable to survive in a desperate world because of her goodness and her need for love, Shen Te has to invent an alter ego. Only when disguised as her "male cousin," Shui Ta, is she able to resist love and treat people with sufficient ruthlessness to assure her survival. The gods, who have come to earth to find a good person, cannot resolve this situation. Instead, they hurry back to heaven and leave Shen Te, and the audience, alone with the problem. The Epilogue continues:

It is for you to find a way, my friends,
To help good men arrive at happy ends.
You write this happy ending of our play!
There must, there must, there's got to be a way!

In *The Caucasian Chalk Circle* a way is found, finally, to permit Grusha to "yield to the temptation of goodness," to accept love, and to survive. In the course of much social and political upheaval, a crude and cunning tramp named Azdak is appointed to be the local judge. Azdak gets everything backward and reverses the usual procedures of the court by taking from the rich and giving to the poor. When Grusha is brought to trial for kidnapping, Azdak declares her to be the true mother because she refuses to risk injuring the child in a tug-of-war with his original mother. Azdak also enables Grusha to marry the man she loves when he divorces the wrong couple. Azdak's reign is brief, however, as the Singer tells us at the play's end:

And after that evening Azdak vanished and was
    never seen again.
The people of Grusinia did not forget him but
    long remembered
The period of his judging as a brief golden age,
Almost an age of justice.

❧ *Invitation to a Rehearsal*

Brecht's theories were, in a number of ways, contrary to those of Richard Wagner (see chapter 13). In the latter's ideal of the *Gesamtkunstwerk,* or total work of art, all theatrical elements were meant to merge together under the direction of a single artist to produce a unified effect. The spell of this work should be strong enough to make the spectator forget the real world and enter the illusory world of the drama. In Brecht's epic theatre, on the other hand, individual elements tend to clash with one another, producing contradictions and inviting the spectator to help create a resolution. One of the words Brecht used to describe this process was *Verfremdungseffekt,* sometimes translated as "alienation effect."* Far from wanting to alienate the audience, however, Brecht wished to involve us in his plays by getting us to participate in the resolution of conflict. This offer of involvement was also evident in his own productions. Brecht's rehearsals were open to everyone, and he asked for comments and suggestions from all present. *The Threepenny Opera* was given its title by a friend, Lion Feuchtwanger, who just happened to drop in on one of Brecht's rehearsals. Brecht's plays can be read in this spirit—as if we are in the presence of a work-in-progress rather than a finished drama. In this way, they can be seen as a reflection of human civilization, which is our work-in-progress.

*Alternate and less literal translations are "distancing effect" and "dislocation effect."

Although his behavior is anything but godlike, the appearance of Azdak resolves the conflict in the manner of a *deus ex machina.* The audience is left to consider whether Azdak might not make a better god than the ones that seem to be presently in power.

In *Mother Courage* and *Life of Galileo* there are no gods, and the protagonists themselves must struggle with the problem of doing good in a bad world. Brecht himself struggled with this problem in both scripts, as he wrote and rewrote the central characters. Although Brecht had hoped that audiences would form their own personal views of Mother Courage's behavior, they have tended to accept the character's choices enthusiastically. Her courage, intended ironically by Brecht, has made her a heroine in the eyes of many. The protagonist of *The Life of Galileo* has met with a similarly contradictory response—from author as well as public. To save his life so he can work in secret, Galileo agrees to confess publicly that his scientific discoveries are erroneous because they are contrary to the doctrines of the Catholic Church. His young friend, Andrea, shouts his disappointment for Galileo to hear: "Unhappy is the land that has no heroes." "No," replies Galileo, "unhappy is the land that needs a hero." As readers of Brechtian drama we are invited to explore this conflict in terms of the realities of our own world.

Antirealistic drama asks us to reach beyond ordinary consciousness, but in contrasting directions. Reading expressionistic drama we extend the range of our *feelings* to include subconscious, irrational, and supernatural experience. Brecht's epic drama, on the other hand, extends the range of our *thinking* to include a more rational and penetrating view of the interlocking mechanisms of history, politics, economics, and morality. The goal in the first case is to reveal deeper psychological and spiritual meanings than is possible in realistic drama while, in the second, the emphasis is on social and philosophical meaning. In a third type of antirealistic drama, absurdism, the struggle for any and every kind of meaning is carried on in the face of mounting evidence that there is no such thing—a situation that provokes both laughter and terror.

Absurdist Drama

> *Theatre of the Absurd: The name given by the contemporary critic Martin Esslin (b. 1918) to a body of dramatic works, mainly French, which arose in the 1950s . . .*
> —Jack Vaughn, *Drama A to Z*

In *The Theatre of the Absurd*, Martin Esslin names some eighteen writers whose work belongs, or is related, to the category of drama he invented.* Interesting critical questions have since been raised as to whether one playwright or another is "really" an absurdist. Esslin himself insists that these dramatists "do not form part of any self-proclaimed or self-conscious school or movement" and that "each has his own personal approach to both subject matter and form." Three of these highly individual playwrights, whose work continues to provoke and delight readers and audiences, are Eugene Ionesco, Samuel Beckett, and Harold Pinter.

Ionesco's *The Bald Soprano*, which premiered in Paris in 1950, is an antiplay, that is, a play which mocks realistic living room drama by emphasizing its banality. The opening stage directions of this one-act play describe the *mise en scène:*

[*Scene: A middle-class English interior, with English armchairs. An English evening.* MR. SMITH, *an Englishman, seated in his English armchair and wearing English slippers, is smoking his English pipe and reading an English newspaper, near an English fire. He is wearing English spectacles and a small gray English mustache. Beside him, in another English armchair,* MRS. SMITH, *an Englishwoman, is darning some English socks. A long moment of English silence. The English clock strikes 17 English notes.*]

*Martin Esslin, *The Theatre of the Absurd* (New York: Doubleday, 1961).

The setting and the characters are so bland, so ordinary, and so repetitive that it doesn't seem to matter how many times the clock strikes. This combination of the repetitive and the irrelevant continues as Mr. and Mrs. Smith entertain Mr. and Mrs. Martin by conversing and telling stories that grow more and more nonsensical. The play climaxes in a frenzy of insignificance and, for dénouement, begins again "with the Martins, who say exactly the same lines as the Smiths in the first scene, while the curtain softly falls."

Ionesco uses the same kind of circular resolution in *The Lesson,* in which a nominally realistic occasion and setting—the Pupil arrives at the Professor's home for a lesson—are transformed into the stuff of nightmares, as the Professor savagely destroys the Pupil. "And every day it's the same thing," declares the Maid, who helps him get rid of the body. As the play ends, another Pupil has arrived for a lesson.

Because they present the reader with images of the irrational, Ionesco's plays might appear at first glance to belong to the drama of expressionism. But, although there are similarities, there are also important differences. One of these differences can be found in the nature of the conflicts. In the expressionistic plays of Strindberg and O'Neill, rational protagonists struggle against irrational elements in their own characters and in the universe. These two aspects of the conflict are clearly separate, and the action contains moments in which the protagonists recognize the situation. In *The Bald Soprano* and *The Lesson,* the protagonists' objectives are to communicate with other characters through the presumably rational medium of language. In the rules which seem to govern these plays, however, it is language itself which leads inevitably to ludicrous or savage irrationality. As the Maid tells the Professor: "Arithmetic leads to philology [the science of language] and philology leads to crime." The objective—communication through language—is also the obstacle. In Ionesco's *The Chairs,* as we have seen (p. 49), the protagonist takes the added step of hiring a professional communicator to deliver his ideas for him. At the end of the play, the Orator faces a stage full of empty chairs. As he tries to speak, we recognize that he is deaf and dumb. Although the Old Man dies believing his message will be delivered and his objective achieved, the resolution of the play leaves us with the conclusion that messages which depend on language are either meaningless or impossible to deliver. And there is a further dimension to this resolution. Does the play itself, which employs language, nevertheless communicate something? Is there a meaning in recognizing the futility of language?

Samuel Beckett, like Ionesco, was born outside France but wrote his plays in French and produced them in Paris. Beckett says he chose French because he wished to write "without style." The simplicity of his scripts, in his own English translations, reflects his desire to avoid the perils of language by making his dialogue and stage directions as clear and simple as possible. (Even so, trouble has occasionally arisen over theatrical interpretation of his plays.) This same clarity and simplicity extends to his settings, characters, and conflicts. In *Waiting for Godot,* Vladimir and Estragon are involved in a situation similar to those found in Ionesco's drama—a self-defeating objective. They are waiting for Godot, but Godot never comes, and may not even exist. In chapter 5 we used these five lines from *Waiting for Godot* to demonstrate the basic elements of dramatic structure:

> ESTRAGON [*he turns to Vladimir*]: Let's go.
> VLADIMIR: We can't.
> ESTRAGON: Why not?
> VLADIMIR: We're waiting for Godot.
> ESTRAGON [*despairingly*]: Ah!

This moment, repeated six times throughout the play, provides the basic conflict. Two other characters, Pozzo and Lucky, come and go but they know nothing about Godot. Toward the end of the first act, a Boy enters to tell them Godot cannot come today but will come tomorrow. The first act ends with this variation of the conflict:

> ESTRAGON: Well, shall we go?
> VLADIMIR: Yes, let's go.
> [*They do not move. Curtain.*]

Even when Vladimir agrees with Estragon they do not go. Some other obstacle is preventing them from going. After the Boy returns in the second act with the same message, the play comes to an end:

> VLADIMIR: Well, shall we go?
> ESTRAGON: Yes, let's go.
> [*They do not move. Curtain.*]

For the first time, Vladimir has taken the initiative in offering to go. But even that is not enough to overcome whatever is keeping them there. This is the final recognition: it is not Vladimir who prevents them from going. At the deepest level, Vladimir and Estragon **want** to go **but** something prevents them from going. And, of course, that something is to be found in the title of the play. They can't go because they're waiting for Godot.

This simplicity of action, however, does not lead to simplicity of meaning. The characters appear before us without the familiar background of realism. Their ages, occupations, socioeconomic status, family relationships and even nationality are a mystery. The significance and identity of Godot are never explained. The setting itself seems to be in limbo. But the absence of this information may focus our attention more sharply on some simple, but difficult, questions. Is it not absurd to wait for something that never comes? How much of our own lives are spent in exactly that way? And, who or what is our Godot?

The absence of character and situational background is also typical of the plays of English author Harold Pinter. His settings and occasions, however, are generally more realistic than those of Ionesco or Beckett. *The Birthday Party* is set in the living room of a house on the English seacoast. The inhabitants of the house—Petey and Meg, and their boarder, Stanley Webber—go about the familiar business of everyday life. They eat breakfast, read the paper, clean up, go shopping, go to work, come home, receive visitors. Petey and Meg are married and both have occupations. He is a deck chair attendant at the beach and she keeps a boarding house, or pretends to. But here the realism begins to fade away. Two mysterious visitors, Goldberg and McCann, come looking for the equally mysterious Stanley. They want to punish him for some offense he has committed in the past and return him to "the organization." In their first encounter, they seat him in a chair, take away his glasses, and begin to interrogate him. Their questions are arbitrary and pointless, ranging from the mundane to the metaphysical:

GOLDBERG: When did you last wash a cup?
STANLEY: The Christmas before last.
GOLDBERG: Where?
STANLEY: Lyons Corner House.
GOLDBERG: Which one?
STANLEY: Marble Arch.

GOLDBERG: Do you recognize an external force?
STANLEY: What?
GOLDBERG: Do you recognize an external force?
MCCANN: That's the question.
GOLDBERG: Do you recognize an external force, responsible for you, suffering for you?
STANLEY: It's late.
GOLDBERG: Late! Late enough! When did you last pray?
MCCANN: He's sweating.
GOLDBERG: When did you last pray?
MCCANN: He's sweating.

Goldberg and McCann have caught Stanley in the double bind of language, which, in absurdist drama, simultaneously promises and denies meaning. Stanley is finally driven mad by a child's riddle:

GOLDBERG: Speak up, Webber. Why did the chicken cross the road?
STANLEY: He wanted to—he wanted to—he wanted to. . . .
MCCANN: He doesn't know!
GOLDBERG: Why did the chicken cross the road?
STANLEY: He wanted to—he wanted to. . . .

Author Finds Audience Absurd

On November 26, 1967, *The New York Times* printed the following public exchange of letters between playwright Harold Pinter and an audience member who had seen *The Birthday Party* performed.

Dear Sir:

I would be obliged if you would kindly explain to me the meaning of your play, "The Birthday Party." These are the points which I do not understand:

1. Who are the two men?
2. Where did Stanley come from?
3. Were they all supposed to be normal?

You will appreciate that without the answers to my questions, I cannot fully understand your play.

Yours faithfully,

Mrs. _____

Dear Madam:

I would be obliged if you would kindly explain to me the meaning of your letter. These are the points which I do not understand:

1. Who are you?
2. Where do you come from?
3. Are you supposed to be normal?

You will appreciate that without the answers to these questions, I cannot fully understand your letter.

Yours faithfully,

Harold Pinter

GOLDBERG: Why did the chicken cross the road?
STANLEY: He wanted. . . .
MCCANN: He doesn't know. He doesn't know which came first!
GOLDBERG: Which came first?
MCCANN: Chicken? Egg? Which came first?
GOLDBERG and MCCANN: Which came first? Which came first? Which came first?
[*Stanley screams.*]

The plot of *The Birthday Party* is relentlessly linear. Stanley **wants** to escape—to "cross the road"—**but** Goldberg and McCann have him trapped. They dispense easily with secondary obstacles presented by the other characters and bend Stanley to their will with a kind of psychological manipulation which resembles the soul murder tactic found in Strindberg. Each of the first two acts begins calmly and builds to a frenzied climax. In the first act Stanley gets a birthday present—a boy's drum—from Meg, although it is not his birthday and he plays piano, not drums. Baffled and disoriented, Stanley marches about the room, tapping the drum. The curtain falls as he stands over the seated Meg, "banging the drum, his face and the drumbeat now savage and possessed." At the end of the second act, Stanley dimly recognizes his own madness as he is caught trying to rape a young woman during a game of blind man's buff at his birthday celebration. In the last act, Goldberg and McCann engineer the removal of Stanley, now a total vegetable, just before Meg returns from her shopping. Unaware of what has happened, she reminisces through her hangover about the previous night's party, where she was "the belle of the ball." Petey, who has been unable to save Stanley, listens glumly.

Pinter's clarity of structure, like Beckett's, does not leave the reader with any resolution of meaning. "Meaning which is resolved, parceled, labeled and ready for export," wrote Pinter, "is dead, impertinent—and meaningless." Instead of opening a door to meaning, the absurdist playwright holds up a fun-house mirror in which we see, in distorted images of human action, both the farcical and terrible possibilities of human nature.

Recent American Drama

> HOSS [*singing "The Way Things Are"*]:
> You may think every picture you see is a true
>   history of the way things used to be or the
>   way things are
> While you're ridin' in your radio or walkin'
>   through the late late show ain't it a drag to
>   know you just don't know
> you just don't know
> So here's another illusion to add to your
>   confusion
> Of the way things are
> —Sam Shepard, *The Tooth of Crime*

Waiting for Godot had its American premiere in 1956 with the great vaudeville clown Bert Lahr in the role of Estragon. The production, which was both an artistic shock and a popular success, created a keen interest in Beckett's drama. His plays, along with those of Harold Pinter, have contributed greatly to a continuing American awareness of the possibilities of antirealism. When Beckett's *Krapp's Last Tape* premiered in New York in 1961, it shared the bill with *The Zoo Story*, a one-act play by then emerging American playwright Edward Albee. The following season Albee's full-length *Who's Afraid of Virginia Woolf?* established his special blend of realism and antirealism in the American theatrical imagination. Individual versions of this two-sided approach can be found in the work of Imamu Amiri Baraka, David Rabe, and Sam Shepard.

Baraka's *Dutchman* is set in a moving subway car, suggestive of the legendary Flying Dutchman's ship which sails the seas forever with a crew of dead men. The two speaking characters are Lula, a white woman, and Clay, a black man. The "dead men" are the other passengers who begin to enter the car in the second scene and eventually throw Clay's body off the train after Lula stabs him to death. These nonspeaking characters fill the dramatic space with their presence, which is both real—subway cars do carry anonymous, silent passengers—and symbolic; like a Greek chorus they link the protagonist with the audience and the society beyond the theatre. When they leave the car after Clay is disposed of, another black man enters. In the final image of the play, a black conductor "continues down the aisle with his little dance and . . . mumbled song. The conductor tips his hat when he reaches [Lula's] seat, and continues out the car." The vision of the future implied by this circular resolution parallels the legend of the Flying Dutchman. Lula and her crew are condemned to ride the subway car forever, murdering black men, with the apparent complicity of the black conductor. Although *Dutchman* is in many ways expressionistic, with its projection of subconscious fears, it also, like a Brecht play, raises social issues and leaves the audience with questions to ponder: What is Lula's objective? Will the next young black resist Lula and save his life? Is any new light shed on racial relations in the contemporary world? What is our role in this world?

David Rabe's *Sticks and Bones* also involves us in a specific social issue, the Vietnam War. The setting is the familiar family living room of traditional realism, but with significant new props representing a timely version of reality—a slide projector, a movie projector, and a "glowing, murmuring" television set. The characters who inhabit this media-dominated environment are the typical American family as presented on television's "Ozzie and Harriet Show." Their names are Ozzie, Harriet, David, and Rick, and their behavior is television behavior:

RICK: Hi, Mom. Hi, Dad.
HARRIET: Hi, Rick.
OZZIE: Hi, Rick.
HARRIET: Ohhh, Ricky, Ricky, your brother's on his way home. David's coming home.

But David's homecoming creates a different kind of situation than is found in situation comedy. Blinded in the war, a stranger in his own family, and haunted by the vision of a Vietnamese girl, David brings a terrifying reality into the artificial coziness of his family's life. The war dead, David reports, are starting to come home:

> DAVID: They're walking from house to house, through the shrubbery, under the trees, carrying one of the dead in a bright blue rubber bag.

But Ozzie would rather watch television, Rick would rather talk about movies, and Harriet would rather go shopping than hear about the dead. The conflict is resolved when the family persuade David to let them help him commit suicide. Rick takes flash pictures and plays the guitar as the family gathers around David and the lights slowly fade. David's hallucinations—which were his reality—are laid to rest as the unreal, real world of Ozzie, Harriet, and Rick is restored. *Sticks and Bones* reflects a world in which reality and unreality are increasingly difficult to tell apart.

Although Sam Shepard is known to most Americans as a movie actor, he began his career as a rock musician and became a prolific dramatist. By the time his *A Lie of the Mind* opened in 1986 he had over forty produced plays to his credit. Ten of these plays won Obie awards—the off-Broadway Oscar—and one, *Buried Child,* the Pulitzer Prize. Generally speaking, Shepard's scripts are of two kinds: those with fourth wall settings and realistic dialogue, such as *La Turista,* and *True West;* and those written for an open stage and in a more poetic language, such as *The Tooth of Crime, Tongues,* and *Savage/Love.* Although all of Shepard's scripts make fascinating reading, we focus, in this brief introduction, on those which combine realistic and antirealistic action.

Sam Shepard's scripts look very much like Ibsen's, with their detailed descriptions of the *mise en scène* set out in careful and clear stage directions. And, like Strindberg, Shepard sometimes destroys the realism of the dramatic space, as in the final stage directions of *La Turista:*

> [DOC . . . *runs straight toward the upstage wall of the set and leaps right through it, leaving a cut-out silhouette of his body in the wall. The lights dim out as the other three stare at the wall.*]

But, although Shepard is clearly not a strict realist, he does exert careful control over the *mise en scène.* In his "Notes on Set and Costume" for *True West* he writes, "The set should be constructed realistically with no attempt to distort its dimensions, shapes, objects, or colors." For the most part, antirealistic distortions in these plays come from surprising juxtapositions of recognizable, everyday behavior.

In *Buried Child* and *The Curse of the Starving Class* we are once again in the familiar territory of everyday domestic life. Shepard's dialogue is sharply authentic, providing immediate empathic connection with the characters. In

Buried Child, Tilden, "his arms loaded with fresh ears of corn," enters the family living room where his father, Dodge, is watching television:

DODGE [*to* TILDEN]: Where'd you get that?
TILDEN: Picked it.
DODGE: You picked all that?
[TILDEN *nods.*]
DODGE: You expecting company?
TILDEN: No.
DODGE: Where'd you pick it from?
TILDEN: Right out back.
DODGE: There's nothing out there!
TILDEN: There's corn.
DODGE: There hasn't been corn out there since nineteen thirty-five. That's the last time I planted corn out there.
TILDEN: It's out there now.

Although the characters are as real as the corn, they live in different worlds. Tilden is apparently able to visit the past, when the family farm was thriving, and is able to bring real pieces of that past—corn, at this moment—into the present. Like Biff in *Death of a Salesman,* he has returned home, after a troubled life out west, to try to find himself and perhaps deal with a secret family crime—the murder of a child. Tilden's ability to bring back tangible objects from the family past provides the terrifying ending of *Buried Child:*

[TILDEN *appears from stage left, dripping with mud from the knees down. His arms and hands are covered with mud. In his hands he carries the corpse of a small child at chest level, staring down at it. The corpse mainly consists of bones wrapped in muddy, rotten cloth.*]

Two dimensions of time merge in the resolution—but both are presented within the framework of a realistic *mise en scène.*

A typical mother-son conflict opens *The Curse of the Starving Class:*

ELLA [*after a while*]: You shouldn't be doing that.
WESLEY: I'm doing it.
ELLA: Yes, but you shouldn't be. He should be doing it. He's the one who broke it down.
WESLEY: He's not here.
ELLA: He's not back yet?
WESLEY: Nope.
ELLA: Well, just leave it until he gets back.
WESLEY: In the meantime we gotta live in it.
ELLA: He'll be back. He can clean it up then.

What makes the scene somewhat more unreal than the usual breakfast conversation is that Wesley is cleaning up the remains of the kitchen door

---

🌿 *Recognition in Sam Shepard's* Buried Child

In *Buried Child,* Vince comes home to visit after a long absence, but no one seems to recognize him. Frustrated, he takes off in his car, but returns home, in the third act, to face the situation. The following scene takes place in the living room of the family farm house. Present are Vince's girl, Shelley, his Uncle Bradley, and his grandfather, Dodge, who is dying.

SHELLEY: What happened to you Vince? You just disappeared.

VINCE [*Pause, delivers speech front*]: I was gonna run last night. I was gonna run and keep right on running. I drove all night. Clear to the Iowa border. The old man's two bucks right on the seat beside me. It never stopped raining the whole time. Never stopped once. I could see myself in the windshield. My face. My eyes. I studied my face. Studied everything about it. As though I was looking at another man. As though I could see his whole race behind him. Like a mummy's face. I saw him dead and alive at the same time. In the same breath. In the windshield, I watched him breathe as though he was frozen in time. And every breath marked him. Marked him forever without him knowing. And then his face changed. His face became his father's face. Same bones. Same eyes. Same nose. Same breath. And his father's face changed to his grandfather's face. And it went on like that. Changing. Clear on back to faces I'd never seen before but still recognized. Still recognized the bones underneath. The eyes. The breath. The mouth. I followed my family clear into Iowa. Every last one. Straight into the Corn Belt and further. Straight back as far as they'd take me. Then it all dissolved. Everything dissolved.

---

which his father has destroyed the night before. The situation is a familiar one. As in *Death of a Salesman* and *A Raisin in the Sun*, family life is threatened by the swiftly changing values and ruthless competition of American economic life. Wesley, like Biff, has a vague but powerful attraction to the old rural values, but his father, Weston, is too out of touch with reality to be of any help, and his sister, Emma, just wants to leave home and live her own life. In his concern for the disintegrating farm, Wesley installs a maggot-infested lamb in a pen in the kitchen. When his father returns home, slightly drunk and carrying a large bag of artichokes, he encounters the animal:

WESTON [*to lamb*]: What in the hell are you doin' here?
[*He looks around the space, to himself.*]
Is this inside or outside? This is inside, right? This is the inside of the house. Even with the door out it's still the inside.

❧ *Character According to Strindberg and Shepard*

> In real life an action . . . is generally caused by a whole range of motives. . . . My souls (characters) are assembled from past and present stages of civilization, bits from books and newspapers, scraps of humanity, ragged and tattered pieces of fine clothing, patched together as is the human soul.
>
> —August Strindberg in 1888, "Author's Foreword" to *Miss Julie* *(English version by Kari Borg)*

> Instead of the idea of a "whole character" with logical motives behind his behavior which the actor submerges himself into, he should consider instead a fractured whole with bits and pieces of character flying off the central theme. In other words, more in terms of collage construction or jazz improvisation.
>
> —Sam Shepard in 1976, quoted by Don Shewey in his biography *Sam Shepard*

[*To lamb.*] Right? [*To himself.*] Right.
[*To lamb.*] So what the hell are you doing in here if this is the inside?

The lamb is real, the son's concern for the lamb is real, the artichokes are real, the father's drunkenness is real—but a man with a bag of artichokes talking to a lamb in the kitchen is unreal. This image could be a dream from the inside of someone's head. But it has been established, in the dramatic action, as an objective reality, explainable in terms of ordinary behavior. An answer to Weston's question can be found in what Hoss tells Crow in *The Tooth of Crime:* "The Outside is the Inside Now." Or, to put it in the context of modern drama, the realism is now the antirealism.

Our examination of modern drama began with Henrik Ibsen and ends with Sam Shepard. We have seen that the reader of modern drama encounters two contrasting and complimentary perspectives: realism and antirealism. Some playwrights rely primarily on one, some on the other, and some combine the two. Perhaps they could not exist without one another, since they address two important human issues: our need to see ourselves reflected in drama as we really are, and our need to become freshly aware of the underlying and overlying forces that make us what we are. Perhaps the tension between these opposites is a primary source of artistic energy for modern playwrights. Henrik Ibsen began his career as a dramatist in the romantic idealist manner of the nineteenth century. In the sixth decade of his life, he developed a new perspective and became the founder of modern realism. Of his last play, *When We Dead Awaken,* written at the age of 71, Ibsen had this to say: "It completes the cycle [of realistic plays], and makes of it an entity, and now I am finished with it. If I write anything more, it will be in quite another context; perhaps, too, in another form." But *When We Dead Awaken* already contained overt experimentation with antirealism. Perhaps this is the other form Ibsen foresaw. But he wrote no more plays.

If, for comparison's sake, we imagine Sam Shepard's career following the pattern of Henrik Ibsen's, he will enter a new phase in 1993, and complete his last work, promising yet another phase, in the year 2014. This speculation raises some interesting questions. What new kinds of drama will we see and read in the twenty-first century, from Shepard's pen or another's? The cycle of what we have been calling modern drama may already be complete. As we read the tried-and-true plays of our dramatic heritage, an equally challenging new world of drama is no doubt in the making.

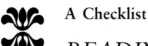

A Checklist

READING MODERN DRAMA

- *What kind of character behavior does the audience see and hear?*
Are the characters the kind of people you would expect to see in everyday family or public life? Or do they seem as if they have been made deliberately unfamiliar? Does the dialogue enhance or destroy communication in the world of the play?

- *What kind of nonbehavioral elements does the audience see and hear?*
When we imagine space dramatically, we imagine the characters' simultaneous behavior in the context of setting. In the modern script, the setting is made concrete and particular, and the idea of setting is extended to include lighting, costuming, props, sound, and music. This combination of visual and aural backgrounds is called the *mise en scène*. Since dramatic space is the crucible of dramatic action, the reader of drama will gain in understanding of the modern play's action to the degree that the details of the *mise en scène* are clearly and vividly imagined.

- *What are the "rules of the game" in the world of the play?*
Do the characters behave, and is the *mise en scène* conceived, according to what is expectable in everyday life? Or does the dramatic action present unusual states of mind, or realities created for this play only?

- *What kind of response does the dramatic action invite?*
Are we asked to enter someone else's dream world? Or see the real world from the inside of someone's head? Are we asked to share insights into historical and political situations? Asked to formulate our own view of social institutions? Does the play point the way to the discovery of new meanings in life, or does it deliberately prevent us from finding meaning in the resolution?

Glossary

The following Glossary contains brief definitions of key terms as they are used in *Reading Drama*. Where possible, the definitions also take into account the way these words are used more generally. Words whose meanings are best understood in relation to other words are treated comparatively in a single entry. All Glossary terms are included in the Index.

Absurdism. See *Antirealism*.

Action. Dramatically intensified behavior, which may or may not be expressed through physical activity. 1. In his *Poetics*, the Greek philosopher Aristotle declares that tragedy is "an imitation of an action," reminding us that drama is made of images of action, and that each individual play can be viewed as having a single, unique action. 2. At another level, action refers to what the individual character does about what he or she wants.

Anticlimax. See *Climax*.

Antirealism. Life seen from the inside, as opposed to the realistic view from the outside. *Expressionism* tends to express one character's inner reality, often in the symbolic language of dreams. The distorted images of *absurdism* dramatize the self-defeating nature of the human drive to communicate. Illusion-shattering *Brechtian drama* (sometimes called "epic realism") demonstrates the connections between political and economic forces and everyday behavior.

Audience. The script presents drama as if it were happening now, in the presence of an audience. The reader can imagine the *responses* of an audience by noticing what kind of role they are given in the script.

Background. The context of action. 1. At the level of the play, background includes setting, occasion, and situation. 2. At the level of character, it includes gender, age, race, nationality, and socioeconomic circumstances.

Behavior. Anything human beings do, whether active or passive, mental or physical.

Brechtian drama. See *Antirealism*.

Character. When action (what the characters want and do) and background (who the characters are) interact with the reader's imagination and empathy to produce the illusion of a living human being. An alternative view of character can be found in the statements of August Strindberg and Sam Shepard (p. 167).

Chorus. A model audience which is part of the dramatic space. All Greek plays include a formal chorus which *responds* to the action at regular intervals. Shakespeare distributes the choral function throughout his cast of characters. Modern drama uses many forms of chorus. Even fourth wall realism, which pretends to leave the audience to its own responses, sometimes contains a choric character, the *raisonneur*.

Classical drama. See *Drama*.

Climax. The point at which dramatic tension becomes so great it must be released. Usually, a series of minor climaxes leads to a major climax in which tension is released for good. In *anticlimax* the release of tension either has no lasting consequences or only happens inwardly to the individual character.

Comedy. A form of drama which seeks to oil the machinery of human society through laughter at antisocial behavior. The main objectives in most comedy are to marry the right young men to the right young women, reform or outwit cranky members of the older generation, and infuse the social contract with love, prosperity, and joyful celebration. There are numerous kinds of comedy, but the *comedy of manners* is the foundation for most. Shakespearean comedy includes comedy-of-manners elements, but in a setting which represents an idyllic blend of the natural and cosmic worlds. Another important variant is *farce*, in which men pursue women, or vice versa, with the emphasis on frenzied activity in the face of proliferating obstacles.

Comedy of manners. See *Comedy*.

Conflict. The clash of a persistent objective with a resistant obstacle. The terms *microconflict* and *macroconflict* express the fact that conflict exists at all levels of the play and should be used in a relative, not an absolute, sense.

Dénouement. The untying of a knotty situation, usually in consequence of a recognition scene or other climax.

Deus ex machina. When a god or superior force shows up at the end and brings the world of the play back into balance and harmony.

Dialogue. In the script, the speaking aspect of the characters' behavior.

Didactic ending. An ending which offers the reader a share of responsibility in solving the social or political problems which create conflict in the play.

Drama. 1. In general, a form of theatre which has become literature, or a piece of literature written to be performed. 2. In the modern era, a kind of play which is neither comedy nor tragedy but has, like real life, elements of both. 3. Images of action presented as if they were happening now, whether on the stage, on film, on recordings, or in print. Two basic subdivisions of drama are classical and modern. From this perspective, *classical drama* includes, but is not confined to, the plays of ancient Greece, Shakespearean drama, and the neoclassical drama of the seventeenth and eighteenth centuries. *Modern drama* begins in the latter half of the nineteenth century. The historical gap left by this method of division represents a period of transition from the classical to the modern world.

Dramatic space. When we imagine the simultaneous behavior of dramatic characters in a given setting or a specific *mise en scène,* we are imagining dramatic space.

Empathy. The human ability to connect with the behavior of others, whether we approve of them or not.

Expressionism. See *Antirealism.*

Farce. See *Comedy.*

Fourth wall. A dramatic convention which asks us to pretend we are witnessing the action through a transparent wall. Originally used in realistic plays written for theatres in which the audience watched the actors through a large opening, the *proscenium* arch.

French scene. When each change in "who's there?" is indicated in the script as a new scene.

Linear and mosaic. Two ways of assembling a plot, best seen in contrast with one another, and sometimes blended in a single play. Linear plots tend to line up and add up. *Mosaic* plots tend to circle around and accumulate. Characters in the linear plot all tend to relate to the same situation, and there is usually a single protagonist (although a group may also function as a protagonist). In the mosaic plot, characters tend to live in their own worlds, forming an ensemble without a protagonist.

Macroconflict. See *Conflict.*

Meaning. The resolution of tension between the illusory world of the play and the real world of the reader. Readers with differing realities will find differing meanings in the same play.

Melodrama. See *Tragedy.*

Microconflict. See *Conflict.*

Mise en scène. 1. For the reader of modern drama, the specific elements of the physical environment which the playwright has imagined and set down in stage directions. *Mise en scène,* in this sense, does not apply to classical scripts. 2. For the producer or playgoer, the *mise en scène* is the total visual realization of any play in a specific production.

Modern drama. See *Drama.*

Mosaic. See *Linear and mosaic.*

Objective. What the character wants. Also project, intention, purpose, motivation. The word *action* is also sometimes used in the limited sense of objective.

Obstacle. What stands in the character's way. The obstacle may be inside or outside the character, and is often another character.

Occasion. A recognizable activity which tells us what kind of expectable behavior the characters are engaged in. When occasions are interrupted by something new or something wrong, a situation is created.

Platform stage. In contrast with the fourth wall convention of the proscenium theatre were the open stages of the Greeks and Shakespeare. Here the audience partly surrounded the actors and were more clearly a part of the performance. Shakespeare's stage was called a platform or *thrust stage,* and has often been adapted for modern use.

Play. A pattern of images of action, designed and assembled by the playwright.

Plot. A pattern of microconflicts which, in time, reveals or expresses a macroconflict.

Proscenium. See *Fourth wall.*

Protagonist. 1. Technically, the character whose pursuit of an objective creates the play's central conflict. 2. Also used to indicate the main character, however this character functions in the conflict.

Realism. 1. The drama of life as it is, a reaction against the idealistic drama of life as it should be. 2. In another context, realism can be said to present the surface of everyday life, in contrast with the various forms of anti-realism, which offer a more subjective or penetrating view. Many modern plays are a blend of both approaches.

Recognition scene. When characters face a truth about the past, the future, life, death, themselves, or others. This is often the moment of final show-down between objective and obstacle, when protagonists recognize truths, usually about themselves and their actions. A protagonist's circumstances are sometimes radically reversed in the recognition scene. In Greek tragedy the *reversal*, or *peripeteia*, is an intense moment in which the extremes of human possibility are momentarily envisioned.

Resolution. When everything is settled at the end. The resolution of classical drama implies the restoration or establishment of an ideal world. Modern resolutions tend to imply that the world is not ideal, or that life goes on more or less the same.

Response. See *Audience, Chorus.*

Reversal. See *Recognition scene.*

Script. The traditional format of written drama, consisting of dialogue and stage directions.

Setting. Where the characters are, physically. Setting may or may not be expressed through specific and elaborate scenery.

Situation. What's new or what's wrong. The situation either can disrupt the occasion or simmer beneath the surface.

Stage directions. In the script, descriptions of background and behavior.

Theatre. A kind of public event in which live performers present themselves to an audience in a single, unified space. Drama, when performed, becomes theatre. It can also become theatre in the imagination, when read.

Thrust stage. See *Platform stage.*

Tragedy.   In its original Greek form, tragedy was drama which depicted a public struggle between larger-than-life protagonists and universal forces. Greek tragedy has been adapted in various ways by other cultures, notably the Romans, the Elizabethans, and the French neoclassicists. Modern drama, especially French, includes much experimentation with the tragic tradition. "Common man" tragedy features the private struggles of ordinary people, in conflict with themselves or with society. *Melodrama,* highly popular in the nineteenth century and in much contemporary film and television drama, attempts to generate tragic power through extreme contrasts in good and evil behavior. *Tragicomedy,* practiced throughout the history of drama, offers happy and often romantic endings to tragic situations.

Tragicomedy.   See *Tragedy.*

Credits

Index of Plays, Playwrights, and Glossary Terms

Play entries include last name of author and date of first performance or publication, whichever is earlier. Playwright entries inlcude nationality, dates of birth and death, and references to pages on which the author is mentioned without regard to a specific work.